INDULGENT EATS

AT HOME

60 CRAVE-WORTHY **RECIPES**

Inspired by the World's Most
Instagram-Famous Food

JEN BALISI

Creator of
Indulgent Eats

PAGE STREET
PUBLISHING CO.

PAGE STREET
PUBLISHING CO.

First published in 2022 by
Page Street Publishing Co.
27 Congress Street, Suite 1511
Salem, MA 01970
www.pagestreetpublishing.com

Distributed by Macmillan, sales in Canada by The Canadian Manda Group.

26   25   24   23   22   1 2 3 4 5

ISBN-13: 978-1-64567-410-8
ISBN-10: 1-64567-410-X

Library of Congress Control Number: 2021931947

Cover and book design by Kylie Alexander for Page Street Publishing Co.
Photography by Jen Balisi, Derry Ainsworth and Stanley Cheng

Printed and bound in the United States

PAGE STREET
PUBLISHING CO.

Page Street Publishing protects our planet by donating to nonprofits like
The Trustees, which focuses on local land conservation.

dedication

To Mike, Mom, Dad and Josa—without you,
this book (and life) would be impossible. I love you.

contents

Pockets of Love   171

Sweet Tooth   197

Be Prepared   219

Introduction

If 2020 taught us anything, it's that there are so many things in life worth cherishing. And that's especially the case when it comes to food. Pizza will always love you; soup has the power to heal so many of life's ailments; desserts will be there for you when you're stressed; and the memories made around the dinner table with a home-cooked meal and good company are among those things we treasure the most. That's the spirit I want to bring to you with this cookbook—a passion that has guided me my entire life.

My parents, who had immigrated to the U.S. from the Philippines when I was born, made sure my sister and I sat down at the dinner table with them every single night. We'd watch *Jeopardy!* and *Wheel of Fortune* while eating plates of white rice with whatever they cooked that night: fried whole fish with a sweet and sour escabeche, oxtails slow-cooked in peanut sauce and chicken braised in soy sauce and vinegar, or adobo, which you'll find later in this book.

Family gatherings meant buffet lines of aluminum trays filled with lumpia (spring rolls), bright purple desserts made with ube (purple yam) and, if we were lucky, a whole roasted lechon (suckling pig). On Sundays, we'd rotate between the local dim sum restaurant and chains like Benihana and Olive Garden in my hometown of Union, New Jersey, which is just 30 minutes outside of New York City. Despite how inauthentic these Chinese, Japanese and Italian restaurants were, these cuisines became my favorites, and the ones you'll see most represented in this cookbook. But it was my 10 years of exploring the diversity of New York City's food scene, coupled with my travels across the globe, the unparalleled influence of the late and great Anthony Bourdain and a move to Hong Kong in 2017 that laid the foundation for my blog Indulgent Eats and the recipes and stories you'll find within these pages.

I discovered entirely new cuisines and dishes, from 3 Michelin–starred meals to street food stalls in small back alleys. I indulged in way too much food for my petite 5-foot (152-cm)-tall stature, hungry to taste as many different flavor profiles and texture combinations as possible. My burgeoning Instagram following (369K at the time of writing) granted me access to kitchens to learn how dishes were made and exposure to the greatest minds in the food world. And yet, in having so many wide and disparate experiences, I also found so many similarities.

Every culture has their version of dumplings, fried chicken, crispy rice, flatbread—the list goes on. This is a theme you'll see in this cookbook, where I've grouped recipes based on the type of food to make those connections across cuisines ever apparent. Social media itself has helped bridge the gap across cultures like no other. Dishes that we originally could only eat through our Instagram feeds have made their way from market stalls across the globe to suburban towns near you. But in case something hasn't made its way to your neighborhood yet, this cookbook will also show you how to make some of these viral dishes so you can let your taste buds take flight without having to leave your home.

This cookbook is all about amplifying the world's most pleasure-inducing foods and the chefs and experts around the world who are behind those dishes. I've highlighted the dining or travel experiences that inspired each recipe and have even guided you to other creators who you should follow for a deeper dive into the various cuisines.

While I've included ways to adjust all the recipes to your taste, this cookbook was ultimately made for people like me who:

- Love big, bold flavors
- Aren't afraid to try new things
- Double the garlic in recipes
- Are addicted to spicy food
- Have a fridge full of condiments
- Add lemon, lime, vinegar or pickles to most dishes
- Value the payoff of cooking low and slow for hours
- Value quick and easy recipes for when life gets busy
- Prefer their desserts to be not too sweet
- Know how to have fun in the kitchen!

Indeed, at the end of the day I truly want you to have FUN. Go ahead and get messy as you roll out dough. Pretend to be a Spartan warrior as you hold up a splatter shield or lid to guard you from any pops of oil while deep-frying. Compete to have the longest noodle or cheese-pull. Gather friends or family around the table to pleat dumplings or share big pans filled with food. And, it should go without saying, that this food is MADE to be shared, both physically and on social media. Be sure to tag @IndulgentEats and #IndulgentEatsatHome along with any related hashtags for the dish (which I've included for every recipe!). I cannot WAIT to see your creations and hope you love them as much as I do.

Let's Get Digital

While this IS a physical cookbook, it wouldn't be an Indulgent Eats cookbook without having a digital component. That's why you'll see a QR code for every recipe, which will bring you to that recipe's dedicated page on my website. There you'll find relevant videos to show you how to make a dish, the original Instagram posts or YouTube videos from the restaurants around the world that inspired it and links to buy any special ingredients or equipment.

These pages also act as a digital FAQ—feel free to leave a comment with any questions you have, as well as any adjustments or unique twists you put on the dish. Since the comments are public, I can answer any common questions and you can also find inspiration from other readers on how they customized different dishes.

Below is a QR code that leads to my digital hub, which has links to each of the recipe pages for easy reference. If for any reason a QR code doesn't work, you can also access this hub at indulgenteats.com/cookbook/letsgetdigital.

Scan this QR code to visit my digital cookbook hub:

Do The Yolky Pokey

I am NOT a morning person. Some days I'm barely capable of waking up
at 11 a.m., especially coming off a late-night editing session for the videos you
see on my Instagram account. But I do crave breakfast every hour of every day,
especially when it involves a perfectly runny egg yolk. While it's not everyone's
cup of tea, there's nothing more satisfying than when I can #DoTheYolkyPokey
and let that rich, velvety egg yolk ooze onto my plate. It's only right that the first
recipes of this cookbook are dishes that I've started my day with more times than
I can count, like the Filipino breakfast (page 19), which I once ate for two straight
weeks in the Philippines. This dish is likely the reason for my obsession with
eggs, which I've featured in every single one of my breakfast recipes
(sorry in advance to the egg haters, but you can also leave them
out in quite a few of these dishes!).

You'll get to try eggs soft scrambled in the ultimate breakfast sandwich (page 14),
baked into a pool of gooey mac and cheese (page 23), soft boiled in a comforting
bowl of ramen (page 27) or paired with a flaky Yemenite pancake (page 30),
salt-cured and cooked into a lava of egg custard flowing out of Hong Kong–style
French toast (page 35), swimming in soy sauce as a dip for sweet Singaporean
kaya toast (page 38) and fried alongside jiggly Japanese pancakes (page 42).
This opening chapter is my ode to the versatile egg, and I can't wait for you
to start (or finish) your day with one of these EGGcellent creations.

THE BEST DAMN BEC EVER

Like many New Yorkers, I would start my mornings with a BEC (aka bacon, egg and cheese) from the corner bodega most days, especially after a night of bar hopping. There was something so perfect about the combination of melty cheese, crispy bacon and a fried egg in a squishy but sturdy Kaiser roll. But after discovering the wonders of soft scrambled eggs and caramelized onions in the Fairfax sandwich from LA cult-favorite Eggslut, I realized that simple isn't always best.

After multiple trials, I'm happy to say that this NYC-meets-LA sandwich is honestly the best damn BEC I've ever had. The smoky spicy aioli , buttery avocado and crispy tater tots/hash browns add the right level of richness to the eggs, plus the everything bagel seasoning makes EVERYTHING better. Sharp American cheese is my cheese of choice for a BEC since it's processed to melt perfectly, but you can also use sharp cheddar or smoked Gouda for stellar results. The best part? The whole sandwich comes together in just 20 minutes if you prepare the caramelized onions (page 220) ahead of time—which you should BECause they make all the difference in this breakfast sandwich!

Makes 1 sandwich

Chipotle Aioli

2 tbsp (29 g) Kewpie® mayo

1–2 chipotle peppers in adobo sauce with 1 tsp adobo sauce (substitute with 1–2 tsp [2 g] dried chipotle chili flakes, smoked paprika or other smoky spice)

½ tsp lemon juice

⅛ –½ tsp ground cayenne, optional

1 clove roasted garlic (page 224), optional

Best Damn BEC

2 strips bacon

6–8 frozen tater tots (or 1–2 frozen hash browns)

In a blender, make the chipotle aioli by combining the Kewpie mayo, chipotle peppers and adobo sauce (or whatever you're subbing in for it) and lemon juice, plus the cayenne (if using for additional heat) and the roasted garlic clove, if you have it ready to go. You can make this up to 3 days in advance.

Preheat the oven to 400°F (200°C). Since we're going to maximize the oven to cook, heat and toast several of the sandwich elements, you will need two baking trays that both fit in your oven at the same time; this is especially handy if you're making more than one sandwich. However, you can also use an air fryer if you have one. Simply preheat it to 400°F (200°C), then air fry the tater tots/hash browns for 15 to 20 minutes until crispy, and the bacon for 10 minutes or until crispy. You can do both at the same time depending on the size of your air fryer.

Prepare a tray for your bacon. You'll need a baking tray lined with foil and a wire rack that sits on top to cook your bacon—this method is foolproof for producing crispy bacon EVERY TIME without having to watch over it. Simply lay your strips of bacon across the rack.

Prepare a second tray for the tater tots or hash browns. You will use this same tray to heat the caramelized onions and toast the bun later, so place the tater tots or hash browns in the corner to make space.

(continued)

THE BEST DAMN BEC EVER (CONTINUED)

¼ avocado

1 scallion

1 slice good-quality sharp American cheese, smoked Gouda or sharp cheddar cheese

1–2 tbsp (3–7 g) caramelized onions (page 220)

1 soft sandwich bun, Kaiser roll or another sandwich roll

Soft Scrambled Eggs

2 eggs

1 tbsp (14 g) unsalted butter

Fresh ground pepper

½ tsp everything bagel seasoning

Bake the bacon and tater tots/hash browns on the center rack of the oven—it typically takes 20 to 25 minutes to get super crispy, but since oven temperatures vary and you may have a preferred level of crispiness, start checking it at 15 to 18 minutes. If both trays do not fit on one rack, place the tater tots/hash browns on your top rack and start checking on it at 13 to 15 minutes.

Prepare the rest of the ingredients while the bacon cooks in the oven. Slice the avocado, chop the scallion, preheat a medium-sized nonstick skillet over low heat and get the cheese and spices ready since the next steps will happen quite fast.

After the bacon has been in the oven for 15 minutes, heat the caramelized onions and toast the sandwich buns on the same tray as the tater tots.

Meanwhile, cook the eggs. Scan the QR code to watch this cooking technique. Beat the eggs well with a whisk or immersion blender for about 30 seconds to completely beat the whites and yolks into a solid yellow color. Raise the heat for the nonstick skillet to medium-low heat, then add the butter and melt it, swirling to coat the pan. Next, add the beaten eggs and swirl if necessary to make an even layer. The moment the edges begin to set, use a rubber spatula to push the edges into and over the middle, layering the egg to form a mound roughly the same shape as the sandwich bun but never folding it over so the bottom of the egg is facing up. If you prefer your scrambled eggs super soft like I do, turn off the heat once the mound is formed. Quickly season with fresh ground pepper and everything bagel seasoning, then top with the scallions so that the seasonings and scallions meld with the still runny top of the eggs, which will finish cooking from the residual heat. If you want the eggs to be more set, keep the heat on low through the next step.

Melt the cheese. If you are using American cheese, place it right on top of the eggs—it was made to melt! If you are using cheddar or Gouda, first push the eggs to one side of the pan, then hold one end of the slice of cheese by the corner and lower your hand to let the surface of the cheese touch the pan while you keep a hold of the edge. Once the surface begins to melt, pick it up and place it onto the scrambled eggs with the melted side up to show off the glossy cheese. Cover and let it continue to cook either from the residual heat or with the heat on low until you reach your desired level of doneness.

BEC ASSEMBLE! The bacon and buns should be ready to remove from the oven. Place the bacon on a paper towel–lined plate and dab any excess grease off. Spread the chipotle aioli on both toasted sides of the bun, then build your sandwich by stacking the tater tots or hash browns, scrambled eggs, caramelized onions, crispy bacon and finally, the avocado. Enjoy immediately.

#BestDamnBEC #DoTheYolkyPokey #IndulgentEatsatHome

FILIPINO BREAKFAST
with Longganisa, Tocino and Garlic Rice

Growing up in a Filipino household, my favorite breakfast of all time is silogs, or Filipino breakfast plates that pair a protein like sweet garlicky longganisa sausage or soy-cured beef tapa with sinangag (garlic rice) and itlog (fried egg), so you get dishes called longsilog, tapsilog and the list goes on. I could eat an entire wok full of garlic rice alone—the deeply savory, mildly nutty and salty flavors just make it so irresistible any time of day. When you pair that with a sweet and savory protein and a perfectly runny egg with crispy fried edges, you get a breakfast sent from the heavens.

Here I will show you how to make my favorite breakfast proteins—the aforementioned longganisa and a sweet, cured pork called tocino, *both of which come from Spanish words for sausage and bacon (a reflection of Spain's centuries-long colonization of the Philippines). To make things easier, you can make the proteins ahead of time (see recipe) or find them in the freezer aisle at Asian and Filipino markets.*

Makes 4 to 6 servings

Pork Tocino

12 oz (340 g) pork collar

½ tsp salt

½ tbsp (7 ml) soy sauce

¼ cup (50 g) brown sugar

¼ cup (60 ml) pineapple juice or 7UP

½ tbsp (7 ml) cane, white or apple cider vinegar

2 cloves garlic, minced

2 tsp (7 g) achuete or annatto powder, optional

Cooking oil, as needed, optional

Longganisa Sausage

1 lb (454 g) ground pork

½ cup (100 g) brown sugar

1 tbsp (10 g) smoked paprika

10 cloves garlic, minced

2 tbsp (30 ml) cane, white or apple cider vinegar

Pinch of fresh ground pepper

1 tbsp (17 g) salt

1½ tbsp (15 g) achuete or annatto powder, optional

Marinate the tocino by combining the pork, salt, soy sauce, brown sugar, pineapple juice, vinegar, garlic and achuete or annatto powder in a resealable bag, massaging it to ensure it's evenly coated. Refrigerate overnight to cure the pork, which will tenderize it and infuse it with flavor. You can also store it for up to 3 days in the fridge, or up to 6 months in the freezer.

Make the longganisa by combining the pork, brown sugar, paprika, garlic, vinegar, pepper, salt and achuete or annatto powder in a large bowl. Use a spoon or your hands to mix everything until well combined. Refrigerate the mixture for at least 2 hours.

(continued)

Shape the longganisa. You can divide the mixture into evenly shaped balls to form them into patties, but I prefer to keep things traditional and shape them into logs. To do this, you will need a 6-inch (15-cm) square of parchment paper and a credit card or other sturdy card. Add 2 to 3 tablespoons (30 to 45 g) of longganisa mixture (depending on how big you want the sausages) to the center of the parchment paper, then fold the paper in half over the meat and away from you so the meat is completely covered with paper. Now use one hand to hold down the top of the paper and the other hand to slide the long edge of the card down from the top of the paper down to the meat, gently pushing the meat into the folded edge of the paper so it compacts and forms a log shape. Repeat this until you've used all the longganisa mixture, setting aside the finished sausages in a tray. Refrigerate overnight or freeze in an airtight container so they hold their shape.

Cook the tocino by adding it to a skillet with enough water to completely cover the meat—you can do this straight from frozen, so no need to defrost. Heat it over medium-high until boiling, then reduce to medium and simmer uncovered until the water has evaporated, which will help cook the meat until tender without burning the sugar in the marinade. This takes around 30 to 45 minutes, depending on the size of the pan and how much tocino you're making. Once the water has evaporated, there should be enough rendered oil in the pan, but you can add a bit of cooking oil, if needed. Panfry the tocino until caramelized all over, 1 to 2 minutes per side, then set aside. You can keep it warm while preparing everything else by storing in a preheated 175°F (80°C) oven.

Cook the longganisa using a similar technique as with the tocino to prevent burning the sugar before the inside is cooked. Arrange the sausages in a single layer in a skillet. You can use the same one as the tocino or cook it in a separate skillet at the same time as the tocino, but note that the longganisa will take less than half the time as the tocino. Add enough water to cover the sausages a little less than halfway, then heat over medium until the water is simmering. Cover and cook until most of the water has evaporated. Then, remove the lid and add oil if needed to panfry the longganisa, turning them until they are caramelized all over. Set aside with the tocino.

Now, it's time to make the garlic rice! Grab a wok or nonstick skillet and heat the oil over medium-low heat, then add all of that minced garlic and get ready for your kitchen to smell AMAZING. Cook the garlic while stirring occasionally until it has just turned a golden brown, about 3 minutes. It will continue cooking out of the oil, so you will want to take it out quickly, before it burns and gets a bitter taste. Remove the pan from the heat and separate the fried garlic from the oil while keeping the oil in the pan—I like to pour the fried garlic and oil through a fine mesh strainer sitting over a small bowl, that way the bowl can catch the garlic-infused oil for you to fry the rice in! Set aside the fried garlic in another small bowl while you prepare the rice.

In the same pan, add the garlic-infused oil back in along with the butter (if using) and heat over medium-high. If you're using rice, use a clean hand to grab the cold rice out of the container and break it up into individual grains (as much as possible) directly into the pan. If you're going low-carb with cauliflower rice, simply add the cauliflower rice right into the pan. Stir-fry the rice until heated through—a few minutes for white rice and 5 to 8 minutes for cauliflower rice. You're looking for the rice to turn a very pale golden color, and for the cauliflower to be soft and cooked through. Season it with fish sauce or salt and stir to combine. I like to crisp up the bottom of the rice, so feel free to leave it on the stove for another 2 to 3 minutes without disturbing it to get some crispy rice bits.

(continued)

Garlic Rice

4 tbsp (60 ml) canola or vegetable oil

1 head of garlic, minced

2 tbsp (28 g) butter, optional but recommended

6 cups (1.1 kg) cold, day-old cooked white rice (jasmine rice preferred) or cauliflower rice

3 tbsp (45 ml) fish sauce (or 2 tsp [11 g] salt)

FILIPINO BREAKFAST (CONTINUED)

Fried Eggs

4 tbsp (60 ml) canola or vegetable oil

4 large eggs

Optional

Handful of chopped scallions

½ cup (100 g) chopped tomatoes

½ cup (100 g) chopped red onion

Pinch of salt

Spiced Vinegar

2–4 tbsp (30–60 ml) cane or white vinegar

1–2 cloves garlic, crushed

½–1 chopped Thai bird's eye chili

Fresh ground pepper

Meanwhile, fry the eggs. Heat a nonstick or cast-iron skillet over medium-high heat until it's hot enough for a drop of water to evaporate on contact. Then reduce the heat to medium and add 1 tablespoon (15 ml) of oil per egg—I prefer to cook only 1 or 2 eggs at a time depending on the size of my skillet. Once the oil is shimmering, crack the egg first into a small bowl, then gently pour it into the oil—this will help with making a more evenly shaped egg. If you want a perfectly round egg to put on top of the mound of rice, you can cook the egg in a ring mold. Fry the eggs to your desired level of doneness—I like crispy edges with a set white and runny yolk, which takes about 2 minutes. Transfer the cooked eggs to a plate and set aside.

Plate the garlic rice by either transferring it to a large serving bowl and topping it with the fried garlic, or make it Instagram-worthy by plating each serving like I did. Grab the same bowl you used for the garlic oil (save yourself from washing another dish!) and add a little fried garlic into the bottom, then fill it with a single portion of rice, pressing the rice in to mold it to the shape of the bowl. Place the serving plate on the top of the bowl and position the bowl where you want the rice to be—make sure to leave space for where you're going to plate the meats and egg! Flip everything over, then gently jiggle and remove the bowl to reveal a perfectly round mound of garlic rice. Garnish with chopped scallions, if desired.

Plate the longganisa, tocino and egg around the rice. You can also put the egg on top of the rice. Serve your plate with a simple salad of chopped tomatoes and red onion seasoned with a pinch of salt along with spiced vinegar. To make the spiced vinegar, combine the vinegar, garlic, chili and pepper in a dipping bowl. Get ready to be transported to sweet, savory, garlicky heaven.

#FilipinoBreakfast #DoTheYolkyPokey #IndulgentEatsatHome

THE OG BREAKFAST MAC ATTACK

Since I first baked eggs directly into my mac and cheese in 2016, there have been a lot of duplicates on the internet, so I HAD to show you how to make the OG. This breakfast mac and cheese with baked eggs is arguably THE most indulgent way to start the day. You have velvety egg yolks that flow into a pool of gooey cheese, which I've amped up from my original cheddar cheese base with the addition of smoked cheddar for even more flavor and mozzarella to make it extra melty and stretchy for those cheese-pulls. Then there's the pop of roasted cherry tomatoes to balance out the richness with sweet acidity, and it's finished off with crispy bacon and that sought-after layer of buttered, toasted bread crumbs that melds with a top layer of golden cheese.

This flavor combination brings an upgraded take on nostalgia, but it's also easy to customize. I've made this with buffalo chicken instead of bacon and roasted tomatoes, and have also done a base of pesto-mozzarella with bacon. Try it with Comté and ham to make a croque madame–style breakfast mac, Gruyère with caramelized onions and mushrooms for an earthy vegetarian version or use a Mexican cheese blend and chorizo topped with crushed tortilla chips to spice things up. Just make sure you're using 8 to 12 ounces (226 to 340 g) of cheese each time to keep the right consistency and enough cheese flavor in the sauce. Have fun coming up with your own version of my breakfast mac!

Makes 4 servings

Mix-Ins (substitute with your chosen ingredients)

6 oz (170 g) grape or cherry tomatoes

1 tsp extra virgin olive oil

¼ tsp dried basil

Salt and pepper

6 strips bacon

Breakfast Mac

Pinch of salt

8 oz (226 g) cavatappi (substitute with chifferi, elbow macaroni, fusilli or pipette)

Roast the cherry tomatoes. Preheat the oven to 400°F (200°C). Cut the tomatoes in half and toss with the extra virgin olive oil, dried basil and a pinch of salt and pepper. Spread in a roasting pan and bake for 25 minutes on the center rack of the oven, then set aside.

Cook the bacon while the tomatoes are roasting. Line a baking tray with foil and lay a metal rack over the foil. Lay the strips of bacon across the rack and bake it on the top rack of the oven until golden-brown and crispy, 15 to 20 minutes. Remove from the oven and lay on a paper towel–lined plate to drain the excess grease. Then, chop the bacon into small pieces and set aside.

Meanwhile, cook the pasta. Fill a pot of water about halfway and bring to a vigorous boil. Add a generous pinch of salt to the water, then add the pasta and undercook it to 1 minute less than the package cooking instructions for al dente. Drain and set aside.

(continued)

Béchamel Cheese Sauce

1¾ cups (420 ml) whole milk

2 tbsp (28 g) butter

2 tbsp (16 g) flour

1 tsp mustard powder

1 tsp cayenne, plus more to taste

8 oz (226 g) sharp cheddar cheese, shredded from the block

3 oz (85 g) smoked cheddar or smoked Gouda cheese, shredded from the block (substitute with another smoked cheese, or cheddar, Pepper Jack or another cheese that melts easily)

3 oz (85 g) shredded mozzarella

2 oz (57 g) Parmigiano Reggiano, grated

Salt and pepper, to taste

Toppings

1 tbsp (14 g) butter

¼ cup (21 g) panko bread crumbs

4 eggs

Chopped scallions, optional

Start the béchamel sauce after you add the pasta to the boiling water. Heat the whole milk until hot but not boiling, about 2 minutes in the microwave or over medium heat on the stove. Melt the butter in a small saucepan over medium-low heat, then gradually whisk in the flour, continuing to cook and whisking constantly until golden brown, about 2 minutes. Gradually pour in the hot milk a little at a time, whisking constantly, until smooth. Bring to a boil and stir in the mustard powder and cayenne, then lower the heat and simmer for 2 minutes to finish the creamy béchamel sauce.

Finish your cheese sauce. In a large bowl, combine the sharp cheddar cheese, smoked cheddar, mozzarella and Parmigiano Reggiano. Reserve a large handful to top the mac later. Add the rest of the cheese to the béchamel sauce and stir until fully melted into a creamy cheese sauce. Taste and add salt, pepper and cayenne as desired.

Mix the mac. Add the cooked pasta back into the large pot, then pour in the cheese sauce and stir until the pasta is fully coated. Reserve one strip worth of chopped bacon, then add the rest to the pot along with the roasted tomatoes and stir until just combined. Transfer the mac and cheese to a cast-iron skillet or baking pan and top with the reserved cheese.

(continued)

Prepare the bread crumbs. Melt the butter and toss the panko bread crumbs in the butter to coat. Sprinkle the bread crumbs and reserved chopped bacon evenly on top of the mac and cheese. Bake for 7 minutes.

Prepare the eggs. The reason we bake the mac first is that you want to develop a crispy, golden-brown topping on the mac and cheese, which takes longer than it does for eggs to bake in the oven. Egg whites also generally take longer to set than yolks, so I prefer separating my egg whites and yolks and adding the yolk at the end to keep it as runny as possible. I find it also looks better for photos since the egg yolk sits on top of the egg white instead of being enveloped in it. If you don't care about this, then skip this step. Otherwise, separate the egg whites and egg yolks, keeping each egg yolk inside half of the egg shell or a small pinch bowl—this will keep it from breaking and also act as a spoon to make it easy to drop the yolks into the mac later.

Add the eggs to the mac. Briefly remove the mac and cheese from the oven and use a large spoon to make four wide wells in the mac and cheese. If you skipped separating the egg yolks, just add an entire egg into each well and bake for 13 minutes so the mac and cheese bakes for a total of 20 minutes. Otherwise, fill each well with an even amount of egg white. Bake for an additional 8 to 10 minutes, until the egg whites are almost set. Remove the mac and cheese from the oven and carefully add an egg yolk into each well so the yolk sits on top of the egg white. Bake for an additional 3 to 5 minutes so the crust is crispy, the egg whites are set and the egg yolks are still runny.

Serve the breakfast mac. Remove from the oven and top with chopped scallions, if desired. Let sit for a few minutes before serving—this is a great time for photo taking. Then, use a spoon to break into those eggs and mix the yolk into the gooey cheese and enjoy.

#BreakfastMacAttack #DoTheYolkyPokey
#IndulgentEatsatHome

BUTTER-MISO RAMEN

with Crispy Bacon and Garlic-Chili Tare

Even though I have an entire section of this cookbook dedicated to noodles, I HAD to include a noodle recipe that's all about breakfast. I just love starting the day with a bowl of soup noodles, whether it be instant ramen or the local macaroni soup and wonton noodles here in Hong Kong, especially on mornings when I'm hungover or sick, and even after a morning workout. That warm, electrolyte-filled broth seems to always revive me, coupled with chewy noodles and if time permits, a jammy soft-boiled egg. Here we're doing a riff on miso ramen that has a whole pat of butter on top, which I tried during a trip to Japan's northern city of Sapporo, the birthplace of miso ramen. The frigid winter temperatures there make perfect conditions for skiing, snowboarding and slurping up ultra-rich bowls of butter-miso ramen. To amp up the flavor and breakfast vibes, we're also adding crispy bacon and making a garlic-chili tare (ramen sauce) with the bacon fat (though you can easily omit the bacon to make this vegetarian!). It all comes together in less than 30 minutes to deliver a noodle soup that might just put you back to sleep in a ramen-induced food coma bliss.

Makes 1 bowl of ramen

Crispy Bacon and Ramen Egg

2 strips bacon

1 large egg

1 tbsp (15 ml) soy sauce, optional

1 tsp mirin, optional

2 tbsp (30 ml) water, optional

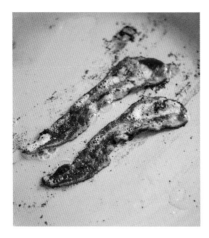

First let's crisp up our bacon! Start with a cold skillet and lay the bacon strips in the pan so they're close but not touching. Cook over low heat for 15 to 20 minutes, flipping occasionally until you get it to the desired crispiness. Let your bacon take a nap on a paper towel–lined plate, but save the bacon grease! We'll add it to the garlic-chili tare, which will provide the flavor, umami and heat in our breakfast ramen. Reserve 1 teaspoon of bacon fat in the pan and strain the rest into a heatproof container to remove impurities and cool, then transfer to an airtight container or freeze in an ice cube tray to defrost and use when cooking fried rice, noodles, pasta and more!

Prepare the soft-boiled egg while the bacon is cooking. In a small saucepan filled halfway with water, set the heat to medium-high and bring to a boil. Then, adjust the heat to low and use a slotted spoon to gently add the egg to the water. Set a timer for 6½ minutes for a slightly runny, jammy egg yolk and a fully set egg white, adding more time depending on how cooked you want the yolk to be. Prepare a bowl of ice water while the egg is cooking so that once the timer goes off, you can use a slotted spoon to transfer the egg to the ice bath to stop it from cooking and also to make it easier to peel. You can also simply fry the egg if you don't feel like boiling water and peeling eggs.

Optional: Make a ramen egg. Make the soft-boiled egg the night before, let it sit in the ice bath for at least 5 minutes to fully cool, then peel it and marinate it in a resealable bag with the soy sauce, mirin and water—squeeze out the air so the egg is fully submerged in the liquid.

(continued)

BUTTER-MISO RAMEN (CONTINUED)

Make the garlic-chili tare. Add the sesame oil to the pan with the bacon fat and heat over medium-low, then add the minced garlic and cook until soft and aromatic, about 1 minute. Add the sake and cook for another minute, then mix in the miso paste and tobanjan. Once combined, reserve a small spoonful of tare, then transfer the rest to the bottom of the serving bowl.

Cook the noodles in boiling water according to package instructions and drain.

Meanwhile, heat the broth in a saucepan or the microwave.

Butter-miso ramen ASSEMBLE! Add the broth to the serving bowl and watch as the garlic-chili tare swirls into the hot broth. Add the cooked noodles, then top with chopped scallions, sesame seeds and/or dried nori, as well as the spoonful of tare (just like ramen shops do!), the peeled and halved egg and a big pat of butter. Get it while it's hot!

#ButterMisoRamen #DoTheYolkyPokey
#IndulgentEatsatHome

Garlic-Chili Tare
1 tsp sesame oil

1 clove garlic, minced

½ tbsp (7 ml) sake

½ tbsp (9 g) miso paste

½ tbsp (9 g) tobanjan (chili bean paste)

Ramen and Optional Garnishes
1 pack ramen noodles, fresh, dried or instant

1½ cups (360 ml) chicken or vegetable broth

Chopped scallions

Sesame seeds

Dried nori

1 tbsp (14 g) butter

SCALLION MALAWACH (YEMENITE PANCAKE)

with Everything Labneh and Lox

Flaky pancakes exist in many forms around the globe. Chinese scallion pancakes use oil to create the layers while Malaysian roti canai and Indian paratha use ghee and add egg to the dough. Here we're using butter to make malawach, the Yemenite Jewish version that's a traditional breakfast for many in the Middle East. It became prevalent on Instagram thanks to restaurants like Reunion in NYC, Bavel in LA and Malawach Bar in Jerusalem's famous Machne Yahuda market. My version combines traditional toppings of grated tomato, boiled egg and zhug (a Yemenite hot sauce), but adds scallions, smoked salmon and a Lebanese yogurt cheese called labneh topped with everything bagel seasoning for a play on my fave lox bagel.

For easier prep, you can use frozen malawach or even Chinese scallion pancakes. I'd recommend doubling the labneh recipe, so you have extra for eating with grilled meats, salads, chips and more. You can also double the recipe for the malawach, change the scallions for roasted garlic (page 224) or cheese to enjoy with dips or scrambled eggs or as a sandwich wrap. Or skip the scallions and enjoy with chili flakes and honey!

Makes 4 pancakes with toppings

Everything Labneh

⅛ tsp salt

16 oz (454 g) whole milk yogurt

2 tsp (4 g) everything bagel seasoning

½ tsp sumac, optional

½ tsp za'atar, optional

Make the labneh by adding the salt to the container of yogurt, carefully mixing it all together. Scoop the salted yogurt onto the center of a clean kitchen towel or four to five layers of cheesecloth about the size of a kitchen towel.

Drain the liquid from the yogurt over the next 12 to 48 hours by using one of three methods. I like to stick the towel/cheesecloth inside a big Mason jar with the ends secured over the opening with a rubber band (as pictured) to keep the labneh suspended midway through the jar. It takes up the least space in the fridge (though you can keep it on the counter for a tangier flavor—the salt inhibits bacteria growth in the yogurt, similar to curing), and the jar automatically collects the salted whey that drips out from the yogurt, which you can use to add flavor and nutrients when making soups, baking bread and soaking nuts (Google it!). Alternatively, you can put the towel/cheesecloth on top of a colander or strainer that sits on top of a deep bowl. If you don't care about saving the whey, you can also tie it to your kitchen sink faucet (but be mindful if you need to use the sink!). Strain the liquid until you reach the desired consistency—I like mine to be like a soft cream cheese, which takes about 24 hours.

Transfer the labneh to an airtight container and store for up to 2 weeks. When you're ready to use it, smear a big dollop onto a plate or directly onto the malawach and top with the seasonings. But first let's make our malawach!

(continued)

Scallion Malawach

2 cups (250 g) all-purpose flour

1 tsp salt

½ cup (120 ml) warm water, plus more if needed

4 tbsp (56 g) unsalted butter, softened

4 stalks scallion tops, optional

Extra virgin olive oil or butter, as needed

In a medium bowl, make the malawach dough by whisking together the flour and salt. Slowly add the water, using your hand to mix it in until a dough forms. Add more water if necessary for the flour to fully combine into the dough. Then, knead the dough on a clean work surface for 5 to 7 minutes until it forms a smooth ball. Alternatively, you can add the flour and salt to a stand mixer, let it run on medium-low with the dough hook while you slowly pour in the water until a dough forms, then let the mixer knead the dough on medium speed for 2 to 3 minutes until smooth. Cover your mixing bowl or wrap the ball of dough in plastic wrap and let the dough rest for 30 minutes.

Prepare a malawach rolling station by getting the butter out of the fridge and dividing it into eight equal pats of butter, letting it soften on the counter. Chop the scallions and set aside until ready to use. Cut five squares of parchment paper about the size of a dinner plate and set aside.

Use your hands to smear one pat of butter all over a cutting board or a clean work surface so it's about the size of a standard cutting board. Divide the dough into four equal-sized balls and place one in the center of the cutting board, leaving the rest of the dough in the bowl, covered.

Roll out the dough into a thin rectangle by first flattening it with your palm, then pushing with a rolling pin from the middle out to the edges. You want the dough to be so thin that it's translucent. Once you have a large thin rectangle, take another pat of butter and smear it all over the surface of the dough. Then, coat the buttered surface with a quarter of the chopped scallions, distributing them evenly.

Roll the dough into one long log by first folding over the long edge closest to you onto itself, then rolling it tightly across your work surface. Take the right end of the log and coil it into itself, rolling it to the left side until you form a spiral, cinnamon roll–like shape. Set this aside onto a piece of parchment paper, then repeat this process with the other three balls of dough until you use all the butter and scallions.

Flatten the malawach between the parchment paper by stacking them directly on top of one another with parchment paper between each pancake, then place a cutting board on top and press down with even pressure until you have pancakes about ⅛ inch (3 mm) thick. Transfer the stack of malawach to a freezer bag and freeze for at least 1 hour or up to 4 weeks.

If using, make the zhug by combining the coriander seeds, cumin seeds, black pepper seeds, garlic, chili peppers, salt, parsley, cilantro and olive oil in a blender. For a more traditional technique that better releases the aromas and flavors of the spices and herbs, first grind the coriander, cumin and black pepper seeds in a mortar and pestle. Then, add the garlic and chili peppers, and bruise and grind them in the mortar and pestle until broken down. Finally, add the salt, parsley, cilantro and olive oil until you have a thick, chunky paste. For a thinner hot sauce, you can add more olive oil. Taste the sauce and add more chili seeds to your desired level of spice.

Prepare the toppings before cooking the malawach since it's best to eat the pancakes hot off the pan. In a small saucepan, soft boil the eggs by boiling water over medium-high heat. Then, adjust the heat to low and use a slotted spoon to gently add the eggs to the water. Set a timer for 6 minutes for a slightly runny, jammy egg yolk and a fully set egg white, adding more time depending on how cooked you want the yolk to be. Prepare a bowl of ice water while the egg is cooking so that once the timer goes off, you can use a slotted spoon to transfer the eggs to the ice bath to stop them from cooking and also make it easier to peel.

Prepare the fresh tomato dip. Finely chop, grate or pulse the tomato in a food processor, then season with a tiny pinch of salt.

Slice the smoked salmon if necessary and roll the thin slices into roses, if desired, for presentation.

Cook the malawach by heating ½ tablespoon (7 ml) of olive oil or butter in a skillet over medium heat. Once the pan is hot, peel off the parchment paper from a frozen malawach and press it into the skillet, cooking for 1 to 2 minutes per side until it's golden brown, pressing to brown as much of the surface as possible. Transfer to a serving plate or keep in an oven preheated to 200°F (90°C) to keep them warm while you cook the rest of the malawach.

Serve the malawach with the everything labneh, smoked salmon, halved soft-boiled egg, zhug (if using) and fresh tomato dip, ripping and dipping or building a taco-like pancake sandwich.

**#ScallionMalawach #DoTheYolkyPokey
#IndulgentEatsatHome**

Zhug (Yemenite hot sauce, optional)

¼ tsp whole coriander seeds

¼ tsp whole cumin seeds (substitute with ⅛ tsp ground cumin)

½ tsp whole black pepper seeds

2 cloves garlic

4 green Thai bird's eye chili peppers or Serrano peppers, stems removed, seeds set aside

Pinch of coarse salt, more to taste

1 cup (60 g) flat-leaf parsley, loosely packed, stems removed

1 cup (60 g) cilantro, loosely packed, stems removed

Extra virgin olive oil, as desired

Recommended Toppings

4 eggs

2 tomatoes, finely chopped or grated

Pinch of salt

8 oz (226 g) smoked salmon

GOLDEN LAVA FRENCH TOAST

Hong Kong is home to the best dim sum in the world, with 3 Michelin–starred restaurants serving intricate creations with the most premium ingredients. But the local cha chaan tengs or tea houses are my favorite way to experience all the steamed and fried Cantonese delights. It's where you'll find the elderly reading the morning paper while enjoying siu mai and char siu bao with tea. It's also where, in some cases, you can get a mix of both traditional and new school Instagram-friendly dishes, as is the case at my personal favorite, Chau Kee. They're famous for their viral molten-centered French toasts, filled with purple taro custard or a golden lava of salted egg custard. The rich, salty-sweet egg custard is typically found in fluffy steamed buns, but here it flows out of the egg-soaked bread that is deep-fried to be crispy and spongy at the same time. The only thing more satisfying than cutting in to reveal the explosion of lava is savoring this buttery combination of textures and flavors, though you can also try it with a simpler peanut butter filling that is popular across Hong Kong.

Makes 1 French toast

Salted Egg Custard (substitute with 1–2 heaping tbsp [18–36 g] peanut butter)

1 (1 tbsp [12 g]) salted egg yolk (page 226), steamed and mashed into a paste

1½ tbsp (22 ml) condensed milk

1 tbsp (15 ml) coconut milk or whole milk

1 tsp milk powder

1 tsp custard powder

2 tbsp (28 g) unsalted butter, melted

In a small bowl, make the salted egg custard by whisking together the egg yolk, condensed milk, coconut milk, milk powder, custard powder and butter until the melted butter has fully emulsified with the rest of the ingredients. Freeze the custard into roughly quarter-sized pieces—this makes it easy to handle so we can stuff them between the bread slices for frying. It works best with silicon ice cube trays so the custard comes out easily, and you can divide the mixture into four small ice cubes. Otherwise, you can freeze them on a small tray lined with parchment paper, making quarter-sized drops that will freeze into pellets. Freeze for 30 minutes to 1 hour until solidified or overnight to make ahead. There's no need to do any freezing if using peanut butter.

(continued)

Hong Kong–Style French Toast

2 slices milk or white bread, square shape preferred

½ tbsp (7 ml) condensed milk, plus more for garnish, if desired

1 large egg

Vegetable or canola oil, for frying

1 pat of butter, optional

Assemble the French toast. While HK-style French toast normally has the crusts removed (and you're welcome to cut them off if using peanut butter), it actually works better to keep the crusts on for the salted egg custard filling, as they act as a better barrier for keeping the custard in. First, press the center of both bread slices to make a well to fit the frozen custard into (no need to do this for peanut butter). You want to leave a ¼- to ½-inch (6-mm to 1.3-cm) margin so the custard stays put in the center. Press the frozen custard into the center of a slice of bread (or spread the peanut butter as shown on the next page), then brush or drizzle condensed milk along the margin of the bread to act as a glue for the two slices. Stack the other slice on top, lining them up to form a sandwich and pressing on the edges to seal—there should be no gaps between the slices if you pressed the custard in well!

In a shallow bowl, beat the egg until foamy and lightly dip all sides of the bread in the egg—you don't want to submerge it too much or else the French toast will be soggy. You can also brush on the egg mixture instead.

Fry the French toast. Normally, you can panfry Hong Kong–style French toast and use tongs to turn it on its edge so every side gets fried (try this with a peanut butter–filled French toast!), but turning it vertically will force the more liquidy custard out through the cracks of the bread and into the oil. We want to keep the custard in place, so it's best to do a quick deep-fry to generate the same crispiness all over while minimizing the ability for the custard to escape from the center of our toast (though, if you want to use less oil, see options 2 or 3).

Option 1: Deep-fry the French toast. Add enough oil to fully submerge the French toast in a deep-fryer, heavy-bottomed pot (like a Dutch oven) or high-walled skillet, heating until it's 350°F (180°C). Then, carefully submerge the French toast in the oil—you will need to use tongs or a spider (or a second basket if using a deep-fryer) to press the edges down into the oil to keep it submerged since it will try to float. Try not to press on the center as you want to avoid squeezing out the custard. Deep-fry for 2 to 3 minutes until golden brown on the outside. Remove and transfer to a paper towel–lined plate and use another paper towel to dab off excess oil.

Option 2: Panfry the French toast. Add just enough oil to fully submerge one slice of bread in a Dutch oven or high-walled skillet and heat to 350ºF (180ºC) (use half that amount of oil if making with peanut butter). Panfry until golden brown, 2 to 3 minutes, then very carefully flip it over with tongs, trying your best not to press on the center since this will force the custard out. If you are making it with peanut butter, you can use tongs to stand the French toast vertically to fry each side in the oil to get the edges crispier.

Option 3: Air fry the French toast. I'm obsessed with my air fryer, and it works incredibly well for French toast (the peanut butter version pictured here was air fried!). Preheat the air fryer to 400ºF (200ºC) (you can do this before you start dipping the French toast in egg), then place the French toast in the center on top of a large sheet of parchment paper with slits cut into it (or use an air fryer parchment liner) and air fry for 4 minutes. Pull the parchment paper out of the basket, keeping the French toast level. Slide a pair of tongs underneath and carefully (and quickly!) flip it over. We're trying to keep it as level as possible so the custard doesn't spill out; I find this more successful when you do it outside of the air fryer basket. After you've flipped it, remove the parchment paper and put the toast back in the air fryer for another 3 to 4 minutes or until crispy. Use a pair of spatulas to lift the French toast out of the basket while keeping it level so the custard doesn't spill out.

Serve the French toast. I'd recommend only drizzling a bit of condensed milk on the peanut butter version, but if you like things sweet, then feel free to add it to the salted egg custard version as well! Finish it with a pat of butter in the center of the French toast, if desired, and cut into the center to reveal the oozing golden lava of custard. Enjoy with milk tea.

#GoldenLavaFrenchToast #DoTheYolkyPokey
#IndulgentEatsatHome

Peanut Butter French Toast

KAYA TOAST with Soft-Cooked Eggs

Get ready to go COCO-nuts for kaya toast! This custardy coconut jam and butter sandwich can be found at kopi tiam or coffee shops across Singapore, where the dish originated. It's the ultimate sweet and savory indulgence, as the kaya toast is often paired with a small bowl of soft-cooked eggs dotted with soy sauce and a sprinkle of white pepper, so you can dip your sweet, buttery sandwich into those runny, salty yolks. The soft-cooked eggs (also known as half-boiled eggs) are similar to Japanese onsen eggs but with a much easier cooking process. Kaya jam lasts up to 3 weeks in the fridge, so you can make a jar and keep it on hand whenever a craving for kaya toast hits you, or to spoon directly into your mouth—zero judgment here!

Makes 1 kaya toast, plus kaya jam for 3 to 5 more kaya toasts

Kaya Jam

4 egg yolks

7 oz (207 ml) coconut cream (standard small carton)

½–¾ cup (100–150 g) coconut sugar or brown sugar, depending on how sweet you want the jam

½ tsp pandan extract, optional

In a medium bowl, make the kaya jam by first whisking the egg yolks together until fully combined. Do not beat them just yet.

Scoop out the thicker coconut cream from the container, leaving the thinner watery part in the bottom. Don't shake the can or carton before using since we want to use only the thicker cream; that way it takes less time to develop the kaya jam. If you did shake the container, you may just need to spend more time cooking and thickening the jam later.

In a medium saucepan over medium-low heat, warm up the coconut cream, sugar and pandan extract (if using), stirring well with a rubber spatula to combine fully. Turn down the heat to low, then use a measuring cup or ladle to scoop out about ¼ cup (60 ml) of cream.

Slowly and gradually pour the ¼ cup (60 ml) of hot coconut cream into the eggs with your non-dominant hand while constantly whisking with your dominant hand to combine. This will help bring the temperature of the eggs up, so they don't turn into scrambled eggs when you mix everything together. Once it's fully combined, do this again with another ¼ cup (60 ml) of coconut cream.

Add the egg mixture into the saucepan and use a rubber spatula to continually mix while cooking over low heat. You MUST keep mixing to maintain the smooth and creamy texture. It will take 5 to 10 minutes to get to the thick jam-like consistency, depending on how thick you want it. Remove from the heat, then transfer the kaya to a clean glass jar or airtight container.

Let the kaya cool until it's safe to eat without burning your mouth, or store it for later—let it cool completely at room temperature first, stirring occasionally to let steam escape, before covering with an airtight lid and leaving it on the counter for up to 3 days or in the refrigerator for up to 3 weeks.

(continued)

KAYA TOAST (CONTINUED)

Prepare the soft-cooked eggs by first taking the eggs out of the refrigerator to let them come to room temperature. Do this a few minutes before filling a small saucepan with 4 cups (1 L) of water to boil—make sure the saucepan has a tight-fitting lid. Once the water is boiling, remove it from the heat and add the cold water to the boiling water, give it a swirl, then use a slotted spoon to gently lower the eggs into the water. Cover the pan with the lid and let it sit for 5 to 7 minutes depending on how runny you want the eggs—the eggs will cook in the residual heat of the hot water. Prepare an ice bath while the eggs are cooking, then use a slotted spoon to carefully transfer the eggs to the ice bath, letting them cool for 5 minutes. Crack the soft-cooked eggs into a bowl and add a dash of soy sauce and white pepper to taste. If any cooked egg sticks to the shell, you can either use a spoon to scoop it out or discard along with the shell.

Meanwhile, make the kaya toast. Toast the bread in the toaster or oven. While the bread is toasting, cut the cold butter into big slices—it will soften with the residual heat of the toast when you assemble the sandwich. Once the toast is golden brown, lay the butter on one slice and spread the kaya on the other, then take the kaya covered slice and put it kaya side down on top of the butter. Cut your sandwich in half or in quarters.

Serve the kaya toast with soft-cooked eggs and coffee, dipping the kaya toast into the molten yolks and soy sauce or spooning the eggs onto the toast, and adding white pepper to taste.

Soft Cooked Eggs (substitute with sous vide or fried eggs)

2 large eggs

½ cup (120 ml) cold water

1–2 tsp (5–10 ml) dark soy sauce

Pinch of ground white pepper, more to taste

Kaya Toast

2 slices milk bread, challah or bread of choice

1–2 tbsp (14–28 g) unsalted butter, sliced

1–2 tbsp (15–30 g) kaya jam

#KayaToast #DoTheYolkyPokey #IndulgentEatsatHome

GETTIN' JIGGLY WITH IT PANCAKES
with Togarashi Maple Bacon

♫*On your mark, ready, set, let's go make some pancakes!* ♫ *Jiggly Japanese soufflé pancakes have taken the world by storm as Instagram helped them proliferate to cafes around the world, with many Japanese chains even opening locations outside their borders. I've had them from Osaka and Tokyo's famous shops, including GRAM and A Happy Pancake, but my favorite versions came from a smaller shop called Benitsuru. There we tried a savory stack for the first time, with bacon, two eggs and hollandaise that perfectly complemented the fluffy pancakes. This is my version of that dish, but with an addictive maple bacon seasoned with togarashi, or Japanese seven spice mix. You can also serve the pancakes with maple syrup or your favorite fruit for a more traditional version of the soufflé pancakes.*

Makes 3 pancakes

Togarashi Maple Bacon

2 strips thick-cut bacon

1 tbsp (15 ml) maple syrup

½ tsp Japanese hot mustard, or substitute with Dijon mustard or other sharp mustard and ⅛ tsp horseradish or wasabi, optional

½–1 tsp togarashi

Pancake Batter

1 large egg yolk

1 tbsp (15 g) granulated sugar

¼ tsp vanilla extract

1½ tbsp (22 ml) whole milk

3–4 tbsp (24–32 g) cake flour, sifted (use 3 for fluffier but eggier pancakes, 4 for a bit more structure)

½ tsp baking powder

Egg White Meringue

2 large egg whites, room temperature

⅛ tsp cream of tartar

1½ tbsp (22 g) granulated sugar

To make the togarashi maple bacon, we're using the good old "wire rack over a foil-lined baking tray" technique. Start by preheating the oven to 400°F (200°C). Lay the strips of bacon across the wire rack, then mix the maple syrup and mustard with a brush or spoon in a small bowl until well combined. Brush or spoon half of the mixture onto the bacon strips. Sprinkle the tops with togarashi. Bake for 10 minutes. Carefully flip each strip over and coat with the remaining maple mustard and more togarashi if you want the bacon extra spicy, and bake for another 10 minutes. Once done, let it rest on the rack with the oven off until you're done making the pancakes.

Separate the egg yolks from the egg whites. You will need 1 egg yolk for the pancake batter and 2 egg whites for the meringue. Place the yolk into a medium mixing bowl for the pancake batter (save the extra yolk to make a Salted Egg Yolk [page 226] or to add onto Abura Soba [page 57]) and the egg whites into a large glass bowl or the bowl of a stand mixer. The mixing bowl and whisk attachment or electric hand blender need to be completely clean and dry. Any oil residue will prevent the egg whites from turning into a meringue, so avoid using plastic bowls or whisks since those are more prone to having oil residue; use glass or stainless steel instead.

Start the pancake batter by whisking together the egg yolks and sugar until they turn a bit paler in color and become frothy, 1 to 2 minutes depending on how fast you whisk. Then, add the vanilla and gradually whisk in the milk until combined. Sift in the cake flour and baking powder using a flour sifter or fine mesh strainer—this is crucial to keeping the pancakes fluffy! Whisk everything together until the batter is smooth and pale yellow in color, making sure not to overmix.

(continued)

GETTIN' JIGGLY WITH IT PANCAKES (CONTINUED)

Preheat a nonstick skillet that has a lid over low heat, as low as your stove can go. You can also do this with an electric griddle or crepe maker on its lowest setting, but you need to make sure you have a tall lid that will fit over the 1- to 2-inch (2.5- to 5-cm)-thick pancakes.

Make the egg white meringue. Beat the egg whites on medium speed until foamy, then add the cream of tartar and continue beating until the egg whites become opaque white. Gradually add in the sugar and beat until stiff peaks form, which should take a total of 2 to 3 minutes from when you started beating them. You can check this by lifting up the beater to see if the egg whites stand right up with stiff peaks that bend over slightly. If you're feeling adventurous, you can even try holding the mixing bowl upside down—the meringue should stay put!

Now let's combine the pancake batter and egg white meringue. Use a rubber spatula to scoop one-third of the meringue into the pancake batter, gently folding the meringue in by scooping from the bottom and folding the batter onto itself until there are no more white streaks, turning the bowl as necessary. Do this again with another third of the meringue, making sure to be gentle as you don't want the meringue to deflate. Once that's incorporated, add the remaining meringue and gently fold until there are no more white streaks and you have an airy batter.

Let's cook the pancakes. Brush the bottom of the preheated skillet with oil or melted butter. If you're using ring molds, you can also brush or spray the inside of the ring molds. It's easier to make these pancakes with ring molds—add a third of the batter into the ring molds (a little more than halfway full), then add a tablespoon (15 ml) of water to the skillet away from the pancakes, cover and cook for 5 minutes or until the tops of the pancakes start to look dry. If you are not using a ring mold, use an ice cream scoop or large spoon to add about a twelfth of the batter (basically a large spoonful) to first form the base of each pancake. Add a teaspoon of water to the skillet but away from the pancake, cover and let it cook for 2 to 3 minutes until the top starts to look dry. Then, scoop on another spoonful of batter right on top of the base, add a teaspoon of water to the skillet but away from the pancake, cover and cook for another 2 to 3 minutes. Finally, add the last spoonful of batter, stacking the batter high, add another teaspoon or so of water away from the pancake, cover and cook for 2 to 3 more minutes or until the top of the pancake starts to look dry.

Gently flip over the pancakes using a thin spatula. The pancake should move easily, if not let it cook for a bit longer. If you are making more than one at a time, use the spatula to carefully slip under the pancake then pull backward with the spatula before flipping so that you flip it back onto the same space on the skillet. This will prevent you from accidentally flipping the pancakes onto each other. Add another tablespoon (15 ml) of water away from the pancakes, cover and cook for another 5 minutes or until golden brown.

Fry the egg while the pancakes are cooking. Heat the oil over low heat in a nonstick skillet until shimmering—cooking over this lower temperature keeps the egg white uniformly white with no crispy edges, which works better for this dish. Crack the egg into a bowl first, then gently pour into the skillet, using a ring mold if desired. Cover and cook for 2 minutes or until the white is set and the yolk is still runny (though feel free to cook longer, if desired).

Serve immediately. Stack the pancakes, placing the egg on top or in between the pancakes so you can add a pat of butter on top. Serve with maple syrup and togarashi maple bacon on the side, and use a fork to break into these fluffy clouds of pancake delight.

#GettinJigglyWithItPancakes #DoTheYolkyPokey
#IndulgentEatsatHome

Fried Egg
1 tbsp (15 ml) oil
1 large egg

Pancake Toppings
1–2 tbsp (14–28 g) unsalted butter or whipped butter
Maple syrup, to taste

Send Noods

There's just something a little naughty about noodles. Whether it's the flirtatious act of twirling a fork into a bowl of pasta, pulling up a hot and steamy length of noodles with chopsticks or pursing your lips to slurp them up, the actions of eating noodles alone are enough to raise your body temperature. Then there's the utter satisfaction of sinking your teeth into those perfectly al dente or chewy bites of carbs coated in creamy, luscious, sticky, glossy or slippery sauce before the flavors finally hit your tongue and . . . you've now reached noodle nirvana. This section is all about giving in to your desires with noodles you'll want to enjoy over and over.

Whether you're single, living with a partner or roommates or a whole house of children, the fact is that sometimes you just want to enjoy the intimacy of digging into your own bowl of noodles whenever you damn well please. So, unlike the rest of this cookbook, almost every single noodle recipe is portioned for solo enjoyment—we are #Send(ing)Noods after all! 😋 Most of these recipes are so easy and pantry-friendly that you can make them at 2:00 a.m. with ingredients you already have, so you can whip them up whenever a craving hits.

This chapter is also about playing around with flavors and ingredients. Unlike other sections, which include authentic versions of dishes from specific cultures, none of these noodle and pasta recipes are traditional. And that's part of the fun! Noodles are the perfect base for toying around with flavors, so feel free to customize these dishes to suit your tastes or let them inspire you to mash up your favorite flavors and dream up your noodle fantasy.

MY FAMOUS SPICY PEANUT NOODS

#SpicyPeanutNoods are the ultimate pantry-friendly companion that come together quickly and disappear in even less time. Since I first shared them in 2019, I've absolutely loved seeing so many people make and remake these spicy, nutty noodles, customizing them with their choice of add-ons or making them allergy friendly with almond butter or sesame paste. The secret to these addictive noodles is the combination of a creamy, nutty spread, the deep complex acidity of Chinese black vinegar and the crunch from both the spicy chili crisp oil and savory fried garlic—all enhanced by a splash of umami-rich soy sauce. The only fresh ingredient you need is scallions. You can substitute for cilantro or skip the fresh herbs—just boil some noodles, mix the sauce, toss, top and slurp.

Taiwanese knife-cut noodles are my favorite since they cook quickly, are wonderfully chewy and the sauce and crunchy bits get stuck in those squiggly grooves. I've included instructions on how to use two popular brands that come with seasoning packets, but I usually toss the seasonings and use my own so I can fully control the sodium levels.

Makes 1 serving

3–4 oz (85–113 g) protein of choice, optional

2–3 oz (57–85 g) Taiwanese knife-cut noodles (can be a generic brand from the Asian supermarket or an online brand like Tseng Noodles and A-Sha—see Note for sauce adjustments) or your preferred noodles or pasta

Spicy Peanut Sauce (double if adding protein)

1½ tbsp (24 g) peanut butter, plus more to taste (substitute with other nut butter or sesame paste)

½ tbsp (7 ml) Chinkiang vinegar, plus more to taste

1 tbsp (15 ml) Sichuan Chili Crisp Oil (page 229—substitute with store bought oil like Lao Gan Ma® or Fly by Jing™), plus more to taste

½ tbsp (7 ml) sesame oil, plus more to taste

1 tsp soy sauce, plus more to taste

Scan the QR code to find links to buy the ingredients and watch how the noodles are made.

Cook any proteins you are using first, since those will take longer than the rest of the noodles. You can simply season with salt and pepper, as you'll double the sauce recipe to coat the protein in sauce.

Cook the noodles in a saucepan or small pot according to package directions, reserving at least 1 tablespoon (15 ml) of noodle water.

Make the sauce while the noodles are cooking. In a bowl big enough to fit the noodles, combine the peanut butter, vinegar, Sichuan Chili Crisp Oil, sesame oil and soy sauce. Add 1 tablespoon (15 ml) of the hot noodle water and mix. Don't worry about it being completely smooth, as it will come together more when you add the noodles.

Note: If you are making this with Tseng Noodles Spicy Sichuan Pepper flavor, omit the chili oil and soy sauce in the recipe. Mix the peanut butter, vinegar and sesame oil with the instant noodle seasonings, then give it a taste and add chili oil and soy sauce, as needed. Alternatively, if you use the A-Sha Noodles Hakka Sesame Oil Scallion flavor, omit the sesame oil and soy sauce in the recipe and use the seasoning pack it comes with, mix in the peanut butter, vinegar and Sichuan Chili Crisp Oil, then give it a taste and add soy sauce, as needed.

(continued)

MY FAMOUS SPICY PEANUT NOODS (CONTINUED)

Optional Garnishes

Scallions

Fried garlic

Chopped cilantro

Sesame seeds

Chop the scallions (if using) and set aside.

Combine the cooked noodles and sauce by using tongs or chopsticks to transfer the noodles directly from the pan to the bowl (save yourself having to wash a colander!). If it's easier, you can drain with a colander. Use chopsticks to mix the noodles and any cooked proteins (if using) with the sauce until it's fully combined.

Taste and add more sauce to your preference—I personally add more vinegar and chili oil than the recipe calls for because I'm a fiend for spicy acidic flavors, but I know not everyone else is. Find the ratios that work best for you and jot them down for next time!

Top with your chosen garnishes and add-ons (if using) and enjoy!

#SpicyPeanutNoods #SendNoods #IndulgentEatsatHome

SMOKY SPICY VODKA FUSILLI

Vodka sauce has taken the world by storm. I grew up having penne alla vodka at red sauce joints in my hometown of Union, New Jersey, and in NYC's Little Italy, where it sometimes had pancetta and/or peas in it. As I got older and places like NYC's Carbone and LA's Jon and Vinny's opened, my brain practically exploded as I was exposed to the best versions of vodka pasta. To date, my copycat recipe of Carbone's Calabrian chili-infused vodka rigatoni is my most popular recipe on my blog, having gone viral on Instagram.

But for my cookbook I wanted to introduce you to a different miracle ingredient to infuse into your vodka sauce: 'nduja (pronounced en-doo-yah). This spicy salami paste adds a rich, meaty, smoky taste to anything it touches. It's made with Calabrian chilis so you're getting the same unique heat as Carbone's version but with the deep savory and salty flavor from the salami. I've also included options for using tomato paste or canned whole San Marzanos since they cook at different times and produce slightly different sauces.

Tip: *Make extra sauce to use for Mozzarella en Carozza (page 71) or Burrata-Topped Crispy Skillet Pizza (page 83). You can also freeze leftover sauce in an airtight container for up to 3 months.*

Makes 2 to 4 servings

For a smoother, quicker sauce

½ cup (120 g) tomato paste

For a chunkier, simmered sauce

¼ cup (60 g) tomato paste

7 oz (198 g) whole San Marzano or Italian tomatoes

Smoky Spicy Vodka Fusilli

1 tbsp (15 ml) olive oil

1 tbsp (14 g) butter

½ medium onion, finely chopped

2 cloves garlic, minced

2–3 tbsp (30–45 g) 'nduja or 'nduja paste (substitute with 1–2 tbsp [15–30 g] Calabrian chili paste or 1–2 tsp [2.5–5 g] crushed red pepper flakes)

¼ cup (60 ml) vodka

½ lb (227 g) dry pasta like fusilli, campanelle, pipette or radiatore

Scan the QR code to watch how to make both types of sauce.

To make a smoother sauce that will cook faster, you will just use tomato paste, along with the rest of the sauce ingredients. Jump ahead to the "Cook the pasta" step.

To make a chunkier sauce with bits of tomato, you will use a combination of tomato paste and whole San Marzano tomatoes in addition to the rest of the sauce ingredients on page 53, and start cooking the sauce first since it needs time to simmer. Heat the olive oil and butter in a skillet over medium heat, then add the onion. Cook until softened, stirring occasionally, 5 to 7 minutes. Add the garlic (and chili paste or crushed red pepper flakes if using in place of the 'nduja) and cook another minute, then add the 'nduja, tomato paste and vodka, cooking until the alcohol evaporates. Add the tomatoes, using your hands to crush them directly into the pan (so cathartic!) or crushing them with a wooden spoon. Bring to a boil then lower the heat and simmer for 15 minutes—you'll use this time to cook the pasta.

Cook the pasta in a pot of well salted, boiling water until a minute before al dente according to package instructions. Reserve 1 cup (240 ml) of pasta water before draining the pasta.

(continued)

SMOKY SPICY VODKA FUSILLI (CONTINUED)

If making the smoother sauce, do this step while the pasta is cooking. Heat the olive oil and butter in a skillet over medium heat, then add the onion. Cook until softened, stirring occasionally, 5 to 7 minutes. Add the garlic (and chili paste or crushed red pepper flakes if using in place of the 'nduja) and cook another minute, then add the 'nduja and tomato paste. Cook the tomato paste mixture until it turns brick red, 5 to 7 minutes. Then, add the vodka to deglaze the pan, using the liquid to scrape any bits stuck to the bottom and cooking until the alcohol smell has gone.

For both types of sauce, add the cream to the sauce by first mixing 2 tablespoons (30 ml) of pasta water into the cream, which helps bring the temperature up so it doesn't curdle when you mix it with the sauce. The starch in the pasta water will also help emulsify the sauce. Once that's well combined, stir the cream into the sauce along with half of the Parmigiano and add salt and pepper to taste. If you plan to freeze any leftover sauce, separate it from the rest of the sauce now—just transfer it to an airtight container with some space in the container to allow for expansion, then allow to cool to room temperature before covering and storing in the freezer.

Add the cooked pasta to the sauce and cook over medium-low heat, stirring while shaking the pan to emulsify the sauce and adding pasta water as needed to get your preferred sauce consistency. If desired, add the cubes of fresh mozzarella when you add the pasta so they will melt as you toss the pasta.

Serve with fresh basil and as much Parmigiano as your heart desires. Just say when! 😋

½ cup (120 ml) heavy cream

⅓ cup (30 g) grated Parmigiano Reggiano, divided

Salt and pepper, to taste

4 oz (113 g) fresh mozzarella, cubed, optional

¼ cup (6 g) fresh basil leaves, torn

#SmokySpicyVodkaPasta
#SendNoods
#IndulgentEatsatHome

UMAMI BOMB UDON

Umami has officially become one of the five basic tastes next to sweet, salty, bitter and sour, but what exactly IS umami? I use this term and umami-rich ingredients throughout this cookbook, as it's frankly my favorite aspect of food, representing that inexplicable savoriness and deliciousness that coats your tongue and makes you salivate. Originally discovered in Japan, umami stems from an amino acid called glutamate that can be produced through fermentation to make monosodium glutamate or MSG, found in everything from Asian snacks to ranch dressing and Cheetos®. Glutamate also naturally occurs in ingredients like soy sauce, seared beef, ripe tomatoes and the stars of this recipe: Parmigiano, mushrooms and miso.

We're using these to make a riff on carbonara that coats chewy udon in creamy sauce made by emulsifying miso, Parmigiano and egg. Add some "meaty" mushrooms (or go ahead and throw in guanciale or bacon) and you have an umami bomb that's as easy to make as it is to eat. If you want to add heat, you can add crushed red pepper or amp up the umami even more by using doubanjiang, my favorite spicy fermented bean paste.

Makes 1 bowl of noodles

1 block frozen or fresh udon

1½ tbsp (27 g) red miso paste

½ tsp doubanjiang, optional (reduce the miso paste by ½ tsp if using)

1 tbsp (15 ml) olive oil

½ cup (43 g) frozen or fresh mushrooms

1 large egg

½ cup (113 g) fresh grated Parmigiano Reggiano, plus more for garnish

1½ tbsp (9 g) chopped scallions

1 egg yolk

Fresh ground pepper

Crushed red pepper, optional

Scan the QR code to watch how to make #UmamiBombUdon.

Prepare the noodles. You can use either frozen or fresh udon, or any noodles you have on hand, but you'll love slurping up those chewy Japanese noodles in this velvety miso-based sauce. Boil water and cook them according to the package instructions, making sure to save a couple of tablespoons (30 to 60 ml) of the noodle water before you drain the noodles and set them aside.

Melt the miso paste by combining it with 1 tablespoon (15 ml) of the hot noodle water in a small bowl; this will thin out the miso paste and make it easier to combine in the sauce. Mix in the doubanjiang (if using).

Next let's cook the mushrooms. I love having frozen mushrooms in my freezer since they're always frozen at their peak freshness, but you can use fresh mushrooms (like cremini or wild mushrooms) or even dried, rehydrated shiitake mushrooms to add the "meaty" component to this dish. Heat the olive oil in a nonstick skillet over medium-high heat, then add your choice of mushrooms and cook for 5 to 7 minutes, until the mushrooms have browned. Don't worry about any excess liquid that develops in the pan—this will add extra mushroom flavor to the sauce!

(continued)

Prepare the miso-Parmesan sauce while the mushrooms are cooking. In a small bowl, beat the large egg, then mix in the grated Parmigiano Reggiano and melted miso until fully combined and set aside.

Add the udon to the cooked mushrooms, tossing to coat the noodles in the residual mushroom oil and water.

Turn off the heat, pour the egg mixture onto the noodles and quickly use tongs or chopsticks to stir the sauce into the noodles while shaking the pan around; this "agitation" process will allow the egg mixture to cook into a velvety sauce instead of scrambled eggs. If you feel comfortable, you can toss the noodles in the pan to do the agitation process instead of using tongs or chopsticks.

Plate your noodles by transferring them to a serving bowl. Using your fingers or a spoon, garnish the noodles with the chopped scallions by forming a ring in the center of the bowl that's about the size of the egg yolk, then carefully place the egg yolk in the center of that ring. Top everything with a generous amount of fresh ground pepper, more grated Parmesan and crushed red pepper (if using). Take a quick photo of your beautiful creation before breaking the yolk onto your noodles and stirring everything together to enjoy.

#UmamiBombUdon #SendNoods #IndulgentEatsatHome

SPICY TINGLY PORK ABURA SOBA

Sichuan spice meets Japanese noodles in this mouthwatering version of abura soba. Translating to "oil noodles" in Japanese, abura soba is a brothless ramen that's also known as mazesoba, but with the addition of the distinctive tableside rice vinegar and chili oil that you drizzle on to your liking. Add to that a rich tare or ramen sauce, velvety egg and chewy noodles, and you'll understand why abura soba became my favorite bowl of noodles after four separate trips to Tokyo, the birthplace of the dish, and why my videos of it always go viral.

While you can find a more traditional recipe on my website (see QR code), this version uses a spicy tingly pork that's my nod to Instagram-favorite Xi'an Famous Foods' spicy tingly beef noodles. Also referred to as "spicy numbing," or ma la in Chinese, this flavor profile is a hallmark of the Sichuan/Shaanxi region thanks to their bountiful spicy chilis and tongue-numbing Sichuan peppercorn. These ma la spices combine with the base ingredients for abura soba to produce supremely flavorful noodles that will make you feel just as warm and tingly inside. 😄

Makes 1 bowl of noodles

Spicy Tingly Pork

½ tbsp (7 ml) vegetable oil

3 oz (85 g) ground pork

1 clove garlic, minced

½ tbsp (8 g) peeled fresh ginger, minced

1–2 dried red chilis, sliced diagonally lengthwise

1 tsp light soy sauce

1 tsp dark soy sauce

1 tsp tobanjan/doubanjiang

½ tbsp (7 ml) Shaoxing wine

½ tsp Sichuan peppercorn, ground

¼ tsp sugar

Tare

½ tsp rice wine vinegar

½ tsp soy sauce

½ tbsp (7 ml) mirin

½ tbsp (7 ml) sake (substitute with more mirin)

½ tsp miso paste, red miso preferred

1 tbsp (15 ml) sesame oil

Scan the QR code for my traditional abura soba recipe, watch me eat abura soba in Tokyo and watch how to make this dish.

Make the spicy tingly pork. Heat the oil in a wok over medium-high heat, then brown the ground pork, using a wooden spoon or spatula to break up the meat. Once the pork is browned, add the garlic, ginger and chilis, stir-frying for 1 to 2 minutes until aromatic. Add the light and dark soy sauce, tobanjan/doubanjiang, Shaoxing wine, peppercorn and sugar, and stir-fry until well combined. Remove from the heat and set aside the pork in a small bowl.

In a small saucepan, make the tare by whisking the vinegar, soy sauce, mirin, sake and miso paste over medium-low heat until the miso paste is fully dissolved. Simmer for 1 minute, then add to the bottom of a serving bowl along with the sesame oil.

(continued)

SPICY TINGLY PORK ABURA SOBA (CONTINUED)

Cook the ramen noodles according to package instructions. Use this time to get your toppings ready. While I've listed most of them as optional, they're highly recommended as they add Japanese umami elements and a unique Sichuan pickled element. You can find the nori, menma and zha cai at Asian supermarkets and linked by scanning the QR code.

Abura Soba ASSEMBLE! Drain the noodles, place them in the serving bowl and add the spicy tingly pork to the center. Top with either the egg yolk or soft-cooked egg, then surround with your choice of toppings. Snap a photo of your gorgeous bowl before poking that yolk and mixing everything together, giving it a taste and adding rice vinegar and Sichuan Chili Crisp Oil to your liking.

#SpicyTinglyPorkAburaSoba #SendNoods
#IndulgentEatsatHome

Noodles and Toppings

1 pack ramen noodles

1 egg yolk, or 1 soft-cooked egg (page 38)

¼ cup (60 g) chopped scallions, optional

2 tbsp (2 g) roasted shredded nori, optional

2 tbsp (16 g) menma (bamboo shoots), optional

2 tbsp (16 g) zha cai (spicy pickled mustard stems), optional

Rice vinegar and Sichuan Chili Crisp Oil (page 229), to taste

BROWN BUTTER SOY GARLIC SPAGHETTI

When I was a kid, I had a phase where I had trouble eating. For some weird reason, I was rarely hungry, totally disinterested in food and would only eat PLAIN spaghetti. No sauce, no seasoning, nothing but cooked noodles. I eventually grew out of it and "upgraded" to eating the spaghetti with butter and salt like many normal kids would. So, it's only right that twenty-ish years later I give you the exact OPPOSITE of plain spaghetti. Here, the perfectly al dente noodles get lathered in a salty, nutty, umami-laden brown butter soy garlic sauce that invokes the nostalgia of buttered noodles but with a very adult mountain of grated Parmigiano and Asian-inspired sauces that are a joyous union of umami. It's just SOY. DAMN. GOOD. 😊

Makes 1 entrée portion of pasta

4 oz (113 g) spaghetti

½ head of garlic

3 tbsp (42 g) butter, divided

½ tsp red pepper flakes, plus more to taste

1 tbsp (15 ml) soy sauce

½ tbsp (7 ml) oyster sauce

2–4 tbsp (12–24 g) grated Parmigiano Reggiano, plus more for serving, optional

Few cracks fresh ground pepper

Handful of chopped fresh parsley, optional

Cook the spaghetti in boiling water to just short of al dente according to package instructions. Use the cooking time to mince the garlic and gather the rest of the ingredients.

In a medium frying pan or skillet, melt 2½ tablespoons (35 g) of butter over medium heat when there are 5 minutes left of cooking time on the pasta. Use a light-colored pan, if you have it, so you can monitor the color of the butter. Swirl the pan every so often so the butter cooks evenly.

Wait for the butter to brown. First it will foam, then the color will turn yellow, then golden and eventually turn a toasty brown with little brown flecks in it after 3 to 8 minutes, depending on how much butter you're using. Adjust the heat to low the moment this happens.

Immediately add the garlic, red pepper flakes and remaining butter to the brown butter, which will prevent the butter from burning. Stir to soften the garlic for a minute, until aromatic.

Add the soy sauce and oyster sauce, stirring to combine. At this point the pasta should be ready. If not, take the sauce off the heat until the pasta is done.

Use tongs to transfer the pasta directly to the pan. You want the residual pasta water to help emulsify the sauce, and by skipping the colander, it's one less dish to wash! Add some Parmigiano to the pan (if using), then stir the pasta into the sauce while shaking the pan over medium-low heat to agitate the pan and emulsify the sauce, adding more pasta water as needed to get the right sauce consistency. If you feel comfortable, you can toss the noodles in the pan to do the agitation process instead of using tongs.

Serve immediately with fresh ground pepper, chopped parsley and more Parmigiano, if desired. Be quick if you're snapping any photos—this is best eaten hot!

#BrownButterSoyGarlicPasta

#SendNoods

#IndulgentEatsatHome

SPICY FUNKY COCONUT NOODLES

We want the funk! Gotta have that funk! Funky fermented foods give an immense depth of flavor to any dish (think miso paste and sourdough bread), so I want to introduce you to Filipino fermented shrimp paste aka bagoong *(pronounced bah-guh-ong) to bring the boogie to these coconut milk–coated noodles. Bagoong is a staple in Filipino cooking, often mixed into both meat and seafood dishes to amplify the flavors of the other ingredients and bring deep savory flavors that just can't be replicated. In this case, we're making an Instagram-worthy bowl of satisfying shrimp noodles that you can whip up easily with pantry ingredients.*

I always keep frozen shrimp on hand since it's the quickest protein to thaw and cook, plus plump bouncy shrimp pair perfectly with chewy noodles coated in a creamy, umami-laden spicy garlic bagoong coconut sauce that's loosely based on one of my favorite Filipino dishes, ginataang hipon. *You can find bagoong online or at Asian supermarkets, but you can also substitute it for other kinds of fermented shrimp paste or even Chinese XO sauce, which will give a spicier, meatier flavor. You can also make this vegan or vegetarian by using vegan butter, vegetarian oyster/stir-fry sauce and roasted cubed kabocha squash instead of shrimp, which is used in another Filipino dish called* ginataang kalabasa.

Makes 1 bowl of noodles

1 serving wheat noodles

1 tbsp (14 g) butter

1 tsp olive oil

2 cloves garlic, minced

1–2 tsp (6–12 g) bagoong or other shrimp paste (substitute with XO sauce or vegetarian oyster sauce), plus more to taste

½ tbsp (7 g) sambal oelek or chili sauce, plus more to taste

Cook the noodles. You can use whatever noodles you have on hand—I love using Taiwanese knife-cut instant noodles for this, as they have this amazing chewy texture and photogenic squiggly shape, but ramen, udon or even spaghetti works too! Just cook them for a minute shy of whatever the package instructions say, as they will cook a bit more when you finish them in the sauce. Once they're cooked, drain them (saving ¼ cup [60 ml]) of noodle/pasta water) and set them aside.

Make the spicy garlic bagoong butter (say that five times fast!) while the noodles are cooking. In a skillet, heat the butter and olive oil over medium-low heat until the butter starts foaming—look for tiny bubbles. Add in the minced garlic and sauté for about a minute, until soft and fragrant. Do a deep inhale of that amazing aroma, then add the bagoong and sambal oelek. Cook for another minute, making sure to combine everything well—I wouldn't recommend trying to inhale this as the spice will hit you!

(continued)

SPICY FUNKY COCONUT NOODLES (CONTINUED)

4 jumbo shrimp, peeled, deveined and patted dry (substitute with roasted cubed kabocha squash)

½ cup (120 ml) coconut milk (freeze the rest of the can!)

½ tsp white pepper, plus more to taste

Salt, to taste, optional

Fried garlic, chopped cilantro and calamansi or lime, for garnish

Next, cook the shrimp in the spicy garlic bagoong butter. Increase the heat to medium and add in the shrimp, cooking them until they begin to change from translucent grey to orange on both sides, 1 to 2 minutes. You'll finish cooking the shrimp in the coconut milk—stir that into the skillet along with the white pepper and let everything simmer until the shrimp are an opaque bright pink and fully cooked through. Taste the sauce and add extra bagoong, sambal oelek, white pepper or salt to your liking. If you're using squash, simply toss in the roasted squash at this step.

Add in the cooked noodles and toss everything together so the noodles get coated in that luxurious sauce, adding noodle/pasta water, if needed, to get the right consistency and glossiness. Transfer it to a bowl and top with fried garlic, chopped cilantro and a squeeze of calamansi or lime. Snap a pic of your beautiful noodles and enjoy!

#SpicyFunkyCoconutNoods #SendNoods #IndulgentEatsatHome

Cheese Please

Cheese might be the most #FoodPorn worthy AND criminal food of them all. Scroll through Instagram and you're bound to find beyond-excessive cheese creations that quite frankly make me mad at social media sometimes. Things like completely impractical burgers drenched top-to-bottom in cheese sauce or pizza weighed down by so much mozzarella that it all immediately slides off as someone holds the slice vertically. Thankfully, you won't find ANY of that here because I love cheese too much to let it pool into a congealed puddle just for show.

My love for cheese runs deep, with pizza being my all-time favorite food. It's the perfect marriage of yeasted dough, tomato and bubbly cheese, so much so that even bad pizza is pretty good—thanks to the wonders of mozzarella. So here, you'll find that powerhouse cheese as the star of two different recipes: one that gives you an extra stretchy, extra Instagram-worthy #CheesePull with a deep-fried mozzarella stick–like sandwich (page 71), and another that simultaneously showcases mozzarella as a classic pizza topping AND in the form of a whole ball of burrata for an over-the-top but totally amazing new age pizza topping (page 83).

Classics like mac and cheese and grilled cheese also get the indulgent treatment, either topped with lobster and cheddar bay biscuit bread crumbs (page 68) or our versatile caramelized onions (page 80). I've also included my version of two of the most Instagram-friendly cheese dishes around—the baked Camembert bread bowl (page 74) and Georgian cheese boats (page 77), which also highlight funkier cheeses.

LOBSTER MAC AND CHEESE
with Cheddar Bay Biscuit Bread Crumbs

I had to start a section about cheese with the most INDULGENT macaroni and cheese I could dream up, so what better way to start us off than with this luxurious lobster mac? Sure, there may be "rules" that say seafood and cheese don't go together, but if lobster mac is wrong, I don't want to be right. Sweet, tender lobster meat pairs beautifully with nutty and salty Comté, a French aged cheese that's often used in croque madames and is one of my all-time favorites. Mix that with cheese-pull-inducing aged cheddar, the umami king Parmigiano Reggiano and a creamy béchamel and you have a delicious mac and cheese base. But now we need the crunch.

I usually add a layer of buttered panko bread crumbs to create the crispy, textural contrast to our gooey mac, but this time, we're leveling up by using cheesy, buttery, garlicky cheddar bay biscuits inspired by Red Lobster®. You can use their store-bought mix to make the biscuits, but once you learn how to make them yourself, it will be hard to go back. Here they become the bread crumb replacement that takes this lobster mac and cheese into the heavens. For a bright and fresh addition to this rich dish, try pairing it with my Peruvian-style Spicy Green Sauce (page 177) for a surprisingly balanced, truly addictive bite.

Tip: Have extra biscuits? Eat them on their own, as a breakfast sandwich bun or stuff them with cooked lobster meat tossed in brown butter (page 60).

Makes 6 to 10 servings of mac and 8 to 10 biscuits

Cheddar Bay Biscuits (substitute with Red Lobster biscuits or biscuit mix)

¾ cup (180 ml) buttermilk (substitute with 2 tsp [10 ml] white vinegar, plus enough whole milk to make ¾ cup [180 ml] liquid)

2 cups (250 g) all-purpose flour

1 tbsp (10 g) baking powder

1 tsp garlic powder

½ tsp salt

¼ tsp cayenne, optional

4 oz (113 g) shredded sharp cheddar cheese

6 tbsp (84 g) unsalted butter, melted

Make the cheddar bay biscuits up to 3 days in advance, or up to 3 months if you store them in the freezer. Preheat the oven to 450°F (230°C) and prepare a baking sheet with a silicon mat or parchment paper. If you don't have buttermilk, mix the white vinegar and whole milk, and let it sit for 5 to 10 minutes while you prepare the rest of the biscuit ingredients. In a large bowl, combine the flour, baking powder, garlic powder, salt, cayenne (if using) and shredded cheese. Whisk the melted butter into the buttermilk mixture, then pour into the flour mixture and mix until just combined and the flour is no longer dry—do not overmix. Scoop the batter onto the baking sheet with a ¼-cup (60-ml) measuring cup or ice cream scoop, leaving an inch (2.5 cm) between each biscuit. Bake for 12 to 15 minutes until golden brown.

(continued)

Cheddar Bay Biscuit Garlic Butter

3 tbsp (42 g) unsalted butter, melted

¼ tsp dried parsley or 1 tbsp (4 g) fresh minced parsley

½ tsp garlic powder

Lobster Mac and Cheese

1 lb (454 g) cavatappi or shells

1 quart (946 ml) whole milk

4 tbsp (56 g) butter

4 tbsp (32 g) all-purpose flour

Pinch of nutmeg

Pinch of mustard powder

Salt, to taste

Fresh ground pepper, to taste

Pinch of cayenne, plus more to taste (optional)

8 oz (226 g) Comté, shredded (substitute with Gruyère), divided

12 oz (340 g) aged cheddar, shredded, divided

4 oz (113 g) Parmigiano Reggiano, grated

1 lb (454 g) cooked lobster meat, claws left whole, tail and knuckle meat chopped into small pieces

2–3 Cheddar Bay Biscuits (page 68), crumbled

¼ cup (12 g) fresh chives, chopped

1 cup (240 ml) Spicy Green Sauce (page 177), optional

In a small bowl, make the garlic butter by combining the melted butter, parsley and garlic powder. Brush the butter onto the tops of the hot biscuits. Save two to three biscuits for the mac and cheese. Feel free to snack on a biscuit while you cook or let them cool and then transfer them to an airtight container.

Preheat the oven to 400°F (200°C) to make the mac and cheese. You will need a large baking pan or casserole dish, but you can also use a cast-iron skillet if making half the recipe.

Cook the pasta in a pot of boiling, salted water for 1 to 2 minutes less than the package instructions for al dente—the pasta will cook more in the oven, so you want to undercook it for now based on how al dente you like your pasta. Drain the pasta, run it under cold water to stop it from cooking and set aside.

Heat up the milk in the microwave or in a small saucepan, keeping it over medium-low heat while you make the roux—you want it hot but not boiling.

Make the béchamel. In a large saucepan or small pot, melt the butter over medium-low heat. Add the flour and whisk constantly until smooth, forming the roux for the béchamel. Continue whisking and cooking for 2 to 3 minutes until the roux is a light golden brown. Add the hot milk, 1 cup (240 ml) at a time, whisking constantly until smooth. Bring to a boil, then lower the heat. Add the nutmeg, mustard powder, a pinch of salt, a few turns of fresh ground pepper and a pinch of cayenne (if using). Simmer for 2 to 3 minutes.

Make the cheese sauce by first transferring the béchamel sauce to the large pot where you cooked the pasta and turn the heat to low. Separate a handful each of the Comté and aged cheddar cheese and set aside, then add the rest of the shredded cheeses and the Parmigiano to the pot and stir until fully melted. Taste the sauce and add salt and pepper to your liking.

Mix in the cooked pasta and lobster meat, reserving the claws to put on top for presentation. Transfer to the baking pan, then cover with the reserved Comté and cheddar, followed by the cheddar bay biscuit crumble.

Bake for 20 to 25 minutes until the crumble is golden brown and the cheese is bubbly. Garnish with chives and let it sit for 3 to 5 minutes, then enjoy. For extra zing, drizzle some green sauce onto the mac and cheese!

#LobsterMacandCheese #CheesePlease #IndulgentEatsatHome

MOZZARELLA EN CAROZZA
with Marinara Sauce

Whether you think of it as a giant mozzarella stick or deep-fried grilled cheese, Mozzarella en Carozza is one of the best ways to dig into this stretchy cheese. Meaning "in carriage," this Italian snack creates a crispy vehicle for the cheese using two slices of bread that then get coated in bread crumbs and fried. Fresh mozzarella is traditionally used, along with regional add-ins like 'nduja or anchovies, but I found in testing that the extra moisture in fresh mozzarella makes it more difficult to work with and produces less of a cheese-pull. So, we're using low-moisture mozzarella to make it as satisfying and Instagram-worthy as possible, with the bonus of being cheaper to make! That said, this tastes even better when fried in olive oil instead of cheaper canola oil—just let the oil cool then strain out any impurities and transfer to an airtight container to reuse the oil.

Makes 2 sandwiches

Marinara Sauce (makes 2 cups [480 ml] of sauce)

2 tbsp (30 ml) olive oil

½ medium onion, finely chopped

4 cloves garlic, minced

28 oz (794 g) whole peeled San Marzano, Bianco or other good-quality Italian tomatoes

½ tsp salt, plus more to taste

¼ cup (6 g) fresh basil leaves, optional

Mozzarella en Carozza

¼ cup (32 g) all-purpose flour

2 beaten eggs

¾ cup (81 g) panko bread crumbs

¼ tsp salt

¼ tsp fresh ground pepper

¼ tsp garlic powder

4 slices white bread, crusts removed

4 oz (113 g) sliced low-moisture mozzarella

1–2 cloves roasted garlic (page 224), optional

2 tsp (11 g) 'nduja, optional

Olive oil or canola oil, for frying

Make the marinara sauce by first heating the olive oil in a large saucepan over medium heat. Add the onion and cook while stirring occasionally until softened, 6 to 8 minutes. Mix in the garlic and cook for another minute before either hand-crushing the whole peeled tomatoes for some cathartic fun or adding them to the pan and crushing with a wooden spoon. Season with the salt, then simmer for 20 to 30 minutes, until much of the liquid has evaporated. Stir in the fresh basil, then add more salt to taste. You will only need about 1 cup (240 ml) of sauce for two mozzarella en carozza, so set aside any leftovers now to cool at room temperature before storing in an airtight container in the fridge or freezer to use for the Burrata-Topped Crispy Skillet Pizza (page 83) or Chicken Parm "Pizza" (page 101).

Prepare a breading station by putting the flour, beaten eggs and the panko bread crumbs mixed with the salt, pepper and garlic powder into three separate shallow bowls.

Build the sandwiches. Press the center of the bread slices slightly to make a well for the cheese, then split the cheese slices between two of the bread slices, trimming the edges of the cheese, if needed, so they fit inside the bread with a little margin around the cheese (feel free to snack on the trimmings!). For more flavor, you can spread a roasted garlic clove or 'nduja on the inside of the bread before adding the cheese. Top each bread slice with another slice of bread and press the edges together.

Prepare the oil by heating a 1-inch (2.5-cm)-deep layer of olive oil or canola oil in a heavy-bottomed skillet until a thermometer reads 325°F (160°C).

(continued)

MOZZARELLA EN CAROZZA (CONTINUED)

Meanwhile, dredge the sandwiches by coating them in the flour, then the egg and finally in the panko bread crumbs on all sides and edges, pressing so they stick and fill in every gap.

Fry until golden brown, 2 to 3 minutes per side. Transfer to a paper towel–lined plate or wire rack, dabbing any excess oil with a paper towel.

Cut in half diagonally to reveal the melty cheese, dip into the marinara sauce and enjoy every bite of that crispy, cheesy goodness.

#MozzarellaenCarozza #CheesePlease
#IndulgentEatsatHome

OOEY GOOEY CAMEMBERT AND CARAMELIZED ONION BREAD BOWL

What's better than cheese and carbs? How about gooey, melted cheese baked inside a big bowl of carbs? Bread bowls are all the rage on Instagram, stuffed with everything from classic soup to more over-the-top loaded mac and cheese, but a baked Camembert or Brie is easily my favorite iteration. It's incredibly simple to execute, but it'll be sure to wow your guests, especially when garnished with sweet and savory balsamic caramelized onions (with prep made easy by using our Caramelized Onion Cubes [page 220]!) and a spicy Calabrian chili honey. Calabrian chili is the star ingredient in NYC restaurant Carbone's viral spicy rigatoni vodka, bringing the perfect balance of heat, salt, smoke and fruity flavor. While it's amazing in pasta sauce and mixed with mayo for sandwiches, we're employing Calabrian chili paste here to bring sweet, smoky heat to our luscious cheese.

Makes 1 bread bowl

½ cup (105 g) caramelized onions (page 220)

1 tbsp (15 ml) balsamic vinegar

¼ cup (60 ml) honey

1–2 tsp (5–11 g) Calabrian chili paste

1 French boule or sourdough loaf

1 wheel Camembert or Brie

2 tbsp (30 ml) olive oil

2 cloves garlic, minced

1 tbsp (15 ml) white wine

Fresh thyme, for garnish

Prepare the caramelized onions by getting them out of the freezer. Let them thaw in a bowl with the balsamic vinegar while you prepare everything else.

Make the Calabrian chili honey by combining the honey and Calabrian chili paste in a Mason jar or bowl. You can find Calabrian chili paste online and in specialty grocery stores, but if you're having trouble finding it, try substituting for 1 to 2 teaspoons (2 to 4 g) of crushed red pepper and a quarter-sized piece of roasted red pepper finely minced. You can make the honey up to 3 days ahead of time—just store it in the fridge and take it out an hour before serving so it can come back to room temperature.

Now let's get this bread ready! A ball-shaped French boule or sourdough loaf will work best for this so you can fit the wheel of cheese inside, plus the fermented flavor of the dough is just right with that creamy cheese. Preheat the oven to 350°F (180°C) while you prepare the bread bowl. Slice the top of the bread off, then cut a hole big enough to fit the wheel of Camembert or Brie in the center. Pull out the circle of excess bread and cut all the excess bread into breadsticks. You can also make long diagonal cuts into the bread bowl in both directions to form breadstick-like cuts in the bread that will be easy to pull apart later.

In a small bowl, combine the olive oil and minced garlic, then use a brush to lightly coat the bread bowl and breadsticks, getting into the diagonal grooves in the bread bowl.

(continued)

Prepare the Camembert by carefully slicing the top rind off the wheel of cheese—this exposes the inside, so it melts properly. Now you can either fit the excess cheese in the bottom of the bread bowl before placing the whole wheel on top of it or just insert the trimmed wheel. Go ahead and snack on the excess cheese. Scoop out a spoonful of cheese from the middle, filling the well with a tablespoon (15 ml) of white wine (drink the rest of the wine while you make the rest of the dish!).

Place the bread bowl and breadsticks on a parchment paper–lined baking sheet and bake it on the middle rack of the oven for about 15 minutes until the cheese has melted and the bread is toasted, then transfer to a serving platter.

Sauté the caramelized onion and balsamic vinegar while the bread bowl is in the oven. The onions will be done when they are warmed through and have absorbed the vinegar.

Plate the bread bowl by placing the onions in a ring surrounding the cheese and garnish with a couple sprigs of fresh thyme. Serve with the Calabrian chili honey on the side so guests can choose if they want to spice things up.

#OoeyGooeyCamembertBreadBowl #CheesePlease #IndulgentEatsatHome

SPINACH AND ARTICHOKE STUFFED CRUST KHACHAPURI (Georgian Cheese Bread)

If NYC's Artichoke Pizza landed in Tbilisi, Georgia (the country), you would get this spinach and artichoke khachapuri! As the national dish of Georgia, khachapuri refers to the category of Georgian cheese breads, from the personal pizza–like mergruli khachapuri to meat-filled kubdari. I'm showing you how to make the most Insta-famous of them all, Adjaruli khachapuri, known as a cheese boat for its shape that's reminiscent of its namesake seaside region of Adjara. It's eaten by tearing off the outer parts of the bread and dipping it into the custard-like sharp cheese filling that gets topped with extra pats of butter and an egg yolk. Mix it all together and revel in the gooey pool of decadence!

Khachapuri is traditionally made with local imeruli and sulguni cheese, but we're using easier-to-find crumbled feta and stretchy mozzarella as many Georgian restaurants in the U.S. do. And while you can leave out the spinach and artichoke, I love the way this invokes the food memories I have of late-night spin-dip and decadent artichoke pizza. We're also stuffing the crust with cheese for even more nostalgia, because when it comes to cheese and khachapuri, the limit does not exist!

Makes 2 (8-inch [20-cm]) khachapuri

Khachapuri Dough (substitute with store-bought pizza dough for convenience)

½ cup (120 ml) warm milk

½ tsp sugar

1 tsp active dry yeast

1 tbsp (15 ml) olive oil, plus more for the bowl

1 tsp salt

2 cups (250 g) all-purpose flour, divided, plus more for dusting

Warm the milk in a saucepan or in the microwave for 15-second increments so we can use it to bring the yeast to life. Once warm, transfer it to a large bowl and mix in the sugar until it has dissolved. Add the yeast and let it sit for 5 to 10 minutes—it will form a creamy, frothy foam on top to let you know it's ready to rock.

Make the khachapuri dough. Add the olive oil, salt and 1¾ cups (220 g) of the flour to the milk and yeast, mixing until a shaggy dough starts to form. Dump out the dough onto a clean working surface that's been dusted with a little flour, whether it be a countertop or a large cutting board. Knead the dough for 3 to 5 minutes, adding as much of the remaining ¼ cup (31 g) of flour as needed until you get the dough so it's tacky but not sticking to your hands. Continue kneading for a couple more minutes until a smooth ball of dough forms. You can also do this in a stand mixer, mixing and kneading for 2 to 3 minutes on medium speed with the dough hook. Transfer the dough to a large, lightly oiled bowl, cover and let it rise for 1 to 1½ hours in a warm spot (like the inside of a closed, unheated oven with a bowl of hot water below it) so that it doubles in size.

If you are using pizza dough, let it come to room temperature by removing it from the fridge at least 30 minutes before rolling out the dough.

(continued)

Make the khachapuri filling. In a large bowl, combine the spinach, artichoke, mozzarella, feta, garlic and egg. Set aside.

Preheat the oven to 450ºF (230ºC) and place a baking sheet on the center rack. For a crispier base, you can also use a pizza stone if you have one. If using, place it in the oven to preheat.

Divide and shape the khachapuri/pizza dough. Punch out the air in the dough, then split it into two equal pieces. Roll each one out into a thin long oval about 8 inches (20 cm) in length, then transfer to a sheet of parchment paper or a silicon mat, leaving at least 5 inches (13 cm) between each khachapuri if you are baking them on a single tray. Fold the long, outer edges of the dough onto itself then roll it toward the center of the oval to form a thick crust. Optional: Stuff the crust with cheese by first adding the shredded mozzarella or the string cheese halves in a thin line along the long edges of the oval, leaving a ¼-inch (6-mm) gap between the cheese and the edge, then fold the edge of the dough over the cheese, tucking it in and rolling it onto itself toward the center of the oval to form the stuffed crust.

Make the cheese boats by pulling the long edges of the crust away from the center to create a wide middle and twisting the ends of the ovals to form the eye-like boat shape. Then, add half of the khachapuri filling to the center of each one, using a spoon to spread it evenly, all the way to the crusts. Brush the crusts with egg wash for a shiny, golden crust.

Bake for 12 to 15 minutes until the crusts are golden brown and the cheese has melted. You can also broil the khachapuri briefly to get the cheese bubbling. Briefly remove from the oven to make a wide well in the center, then crack an egg into each well and return to the oven for another 2 minutes until the egg white has begun to set. If using egg yolks, you can simply add the yolk on top when the cheese is done, since it will cook when mixed into the hot filling. Remove and transfer to a wire rack to briefly cool.

Add a pat of butter and a dash of crushed red pepper flakes to each khachapuri then serve immediately, using a spoon or a piece of the crust ripped off to stir the runny yolk and butter into the gooey cheese filling, ripping and dipping to your heart's content.

#SpinachandArtichokeKhachapuri #CheesePlease
#IndulgentEatsatHome

Khachapuri Filling

1 cup (30 g) packed spinach, chopped, optional

⅓ cup (50 g) canned artichoke hearts in water (not marinated), drained and chopped, optional

1½ cups (338 g) mozzarella, shredded (substitute ½ cup [113 g] shredded provolone for sharper flavor), plus another ½ cup (113 g) to stuff the crust (optional, for extra cheesy stuffed crusts, use 4–8 sticks of string cheese sliced lengthwise)

⅔ cup (162 g) feta, crumbled

3 cloves garlic, minced

1 egg

Egg Wash (optional)

1 large egg beaten with 1 tsp water

Garnish

2 eggs or egg yolks

2 tbsp (28 g) unsalted butter

Crushed red pepper flakes, to taste

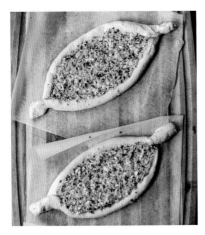

FRENCH ONION GRILLED CHEESE

It's amazing how something as simple as sliced bread, butter and cheese can bring so much comfort. While I grew up with good old Kraft singles sandwiched between white bread, I eventually discovered the wonders of European cheeses and sourdough (which is THE BEST bread for grilled cheese, full stop). I was also introduced to the savory cheese-pull wonder that is French onion soup and thought it would be the perfect grilled cheese to showcase since it's another genius use of our Caramelized Onion Cubes (page 220). We're also using my new favorite way to make grilled cheese that's also gone viral. You start by melting the cheese directly on a nonstick pan, and then stick the bread onto the already-melted cheese before flipping it all over to toast. This saves you the trouble of worrying about the bread burning while you wait for the cheese to melt, and you also get crispy edges of cheese to add texture and depth of flavor. Use this technique whenever you make a sandwich with melted cheese!

Makes 1 grilled cheese, adjust the quantities based on bread size

3–4 tbsp (40–60 g) caramelized onions (page 220)

1–1½ tbsp (15–22 ml) sherry or red wine vinegar

3–4 oz (85–113 g) Gruyère cheese, freshly grated

2 slices thin sourdough or French boule bread (sliced ½ inch [1.3 cm] thick or less)

2 pats unsalted butter

Scan the QR code to see this grilled cheese technique in action.

In a nonstick pan, heat the caramelized onions over medium-low heat. Add the sherry. Stir it all together until the wine has been fully absorbed into the onions, then sauté for another minute.

Add the Gruyère to the pan, spreading it all over the onions. Give the whole thing a little mix so the cheese begins to melt into the onions, then use the spatula to shape the mixture so it's in two mounds, each roughly the size of the two slices of bread.

Assemble the grilled cheese. Press a slice of bread onto each mound so the melting Gruyère glues to the bread. Add a small pat of butter to the middle of each slice, then carefully flip each slice over so the butter is now melting into the pan and soaking into the bread and the gooey cheese and onion mixture is facing up. Use the spatula to turn the slices so they are facing opposite directions with the straight edges next to each other—this will make it easier to flip the slices onto each other so they fit together correctly.

Toast the bread for 2 to 3 minutes, then flip the slices onto each other and press the sandwich together. Continue toasting and flipping the entire grilled cheese until you get to your desired level of doneness. Remove from the heat and let it sit for a minute or two before cutting it in half, giving it a fun cheese-pull, then going to town on your delicious French onion grilled cheese.

#FrenchOnionGrilledCheese #CheesePlease
#IndulgentEatsatHome

BURRATA-TOPPED CRISPY SKILLET PIZZA

FOC YES is what's you'll be saying when you eat this focaccia-style crispy skillet pizza topped with a whole ball of creamy burrata! Pizzerias recently began to use their genius to put an entire burrata in the middle of a pizza, but I've found the thin crust it is usually served on to be too flimsy for so much burrata. To resolve this issue, I'm emulating the thicker crust of my favorite slice shop in NYC, Mama's Too.

Their owner Frank makes the most amazing focaccia-style pizza with shredded mozzarella spread all over the crust to produce a crispy cheese edge. Frank even video-chatted with me to give me pointers for this dough recipe! It creates a supportive base for our burrata (though you're welcome to omit it for a simpler pie). While you can go for a classic marinara sauce (page 71), I've taken inspiration from two other favorite pizzerias in NYC: Rubirosa, with a vodka sauce base (page 51) and basil pesto swirl, and Pizza Loves Emily, with a savory-spicy-sweet combo of pepperoni, jalapeños and honey. If you've got extra cloves of roasted garlic (page 224), then definitely throw those little nuggets of gold on as well!

Makes 1 extra thick skillet pizza or 2 regular skillet pizzas

Focaccia-Style Pizza Dough

¼ tsp instant yeast

1 cup (125 g) all-purpose flour

1 cup (137 g) bread flour

1 tsp salt

¾ cup (180 ml) warm water

1 tbsp (15 ml) olive oil, plus more for the mixing bowl

Start preparing the dough at least one day before you plan to eat the pizza, that way your pizza dough has time to ferment and develop delicious flavor in the fridge. It also helps cut down on the prep time day of, though I'd recommend starting the dough at least 2 days before to really make your pizza amazing.

In a medium bowl, combine the ingredients for the dough by mixing the yeast, flours and salt until well combined. Next, mix in the water and oil with a spoon or spatula until you have a shaggy, sticky dough with all the flour incorporated, then cover the bowl and wait 5 minutes.

No need to knead the dough. We're using a no-knead method that uses time and the yeast's natural fermenting properties to transform the dough into a smooth, air pocket–filled ball. Scan the QR code to watch this in action. Since the dough is quite sticky, use either a bench scraper or a wet (but not dripping) hand to reach underneath the dough, stretching the bottom of the dough out and over the top. Turn the bowl 90 degrees and repeat the process of stretching the dough from the bottom over the top. You'll turn the bowl and stretch the dough over itself two more times to make four total stretches—this process is called creating a fold and helps trap air bubbles inside the dough. Cover the dough and wait another 5 minutes, then use a bench scraper or wet hand to create a second fold (aka four stretches and turns). Wait another 5 minutes, make a third fold, then wait another 5 minutes and make your fourth and final fold.

(continued)

Crispy Pan Pizza Base

2 tbsp (30 ml) olive oil

2 cloves garlic, minced, optional

1½–2 cups (338–450 g) low-moisture mozzarella, shredded

½ cup (132 g) Marinara Sauce (page 71), Vodka Sauce (page 51) or pureed San Marzano tomatoes

Baked-On Toppings (optional)

½ cup (70 g) pepperoni

2 tbsp (17 g) pickled jalapeños (page 223 or store-bought)

Roasted garlic cloves (page 224)

Basil Pesto (optional, makes 1 cup [232 g])

1 cup (24 g) fresh basil leaves

3 cloves garlic

2 tbsp (17 g) pine nuts or walnuts

2 oz (57 g) Parmigiano Reggiano, grated

⅓ cup (80 ml) extra virgin olive oil

Let the dough rise at room temperature for 1 to 2 hours. You can do this by covering the bowl and keeping it in a warm place in your kitchen (like next to a window if you live in a warmer climate), but my preferred method is to keep the bowl in the center rack of a closed, unheated oven with a large bowl or tray of hot water on the bottom rack to help keep a warm, humid environment for the dough. This will help it rise quickly to create the volume we are looking for. When the dough has doubled in size, it's good to go.

Cover the dough and refrigerate it for 12 to 72 hours. Now we're going to slow down the yeast through the process of cold fermentation, which helps to develop delicious flavor in the dough instead of any sour flavors that yeast can impart. The dough will slowly rise in the fridge, so the longer you let it cold ferment, the larger the air bubbles you'll get in the final pizza dough and the better the chewy texture in the crust.

Optional: Divide the dough into two portions. Once the dough is ready, you should be able to get a sense of how thick the final pizza will be. You can keep it as is for one thicker pie (about 1 inch [2.5 cm] thick) or use a bench scraper or knife to divide the ball right in the middle to create two portions of dough for thinner pies (around ½ inch [1.3 cm] thick). If you divide the dough, tuck the sharp, cut ends underneath and into the center of the dough, then place the dough with the tucked-in ends down on a lightly floured cutting board and roll it between your hands to form a smooth dough ball. You can either bake both portions now, keep one portion covered in the refrigerator to continue to cold ferment or freeze the remaining portion for up to 3 months by lightly oiling it with olive oil all around before storing in an airtight freezer bag with as much air as possible squeezed out. Thaw frozen pizza dough in the fridge for at least 12 hours, then leave it on the counter for 15 minutes before the next step.

Coat a skillet in 2 tablespoons (30 ml) of olive oil using your fingers, making sure to get all around the edges, then add the dough into the pan and turn it over to get olive oil on both sides. Press the dough into the pan (with the tucked-in end on the bottom) and start to stretch it out to the edges. If it resists and keeps shrinking back, let it sit in a closed, unheated oven or leave it covered on the countertop for 15 minutes, then come back and try to stretch it again.

Proof the dough in the skillet either in the center rack of a closed, unheated oven for 2 to 4 hours with a large bowl or tray of hot water on the bottom rack, or covered with a kitchen towel or plastic wrap on the counter. This is known as the second rise and it helps to redevelop the air bubbles that were squeezed out when you shaped the dough into the skillet. The dough will look soft and pillowy, begging for you to poke it with your fingers, which luckily is the next step!

Preheat the oven to 500°F (260°C) for at least 45 minutes prior to baking the pizza. You may need to remove the dough if it's proofing and leave it covered on the countertop while you wait, as it shouldn't take more than 10 minutes to build the pizzas.

Assemble the crispy skillet pizza by using your fingers to evenly poke the dough all over, similar to making focaccia. This helps poke out any larger air bubbles for more even baking. Sprinkle the minced garlic over the crust for extra flavor, if desired, then spread half of the mozzarella all over the pie, all the way to the edges. Evenly dollop on your choice of sauce across the dough, leaving a 1-inch (2.5-cm) gap from the edge. Sprinkle on the remaining mozzarella over the sauce. You can make the edges extra crispy and cheesy by using an extra ½ cup (113 g) of mozzarella to make a thick wall of shredded cheese all along the edges.

Choose your pizza toppings. If you plan to use pepperoni (or other meaty toppings), pickled jalapeños and/or roasted garlic, add those prior to baking. Save the rest to add on top when the pizza is out of the oven.

Bake for 20 to 25 minutes on the bottom rack of the oven. If you are baking two pizzas and they both don't fit on the bottom rack, you will need to bake them one at a time, as keeping the skillet right above the heat source is critical for the dough texture. Bake until the cheese is melted and the crust is golden brown (you can peek under with a spatula). If the top needs more time, shift the skillet to the top rack and bake to your desired level, or broil for 1 to 2 minutes to get the cheese on top extra melty and bubbly. If the top of the pizza is done but the bottom of the crust still looks light, transfer the skillet to the stovetop and cook over medium-high until it's golden brown.

Optional: Make the basil pesto while the pizza is baking. In a food processor or blender, blend the basil, garlic, nuts, Parmigiano and olive oil until smooth.

Finish topping the pizza. I recommend letting the pizza cool slightly first, then carefully use a spatula to transfer it from the skillet onto a cutting board so it's easier to cut, though you can leave it in the skillet for presentation, if desired. Top it with the basil pesto (if using) by either using a squeeze bottle or small spoon to make a swirl starting from the center moving outward. Or, add slices of prosciutto, fresh arugula and fresh basil all over. Grate on Parmigiano, then carefully place the ball of burrata in the center of the pizza. Top the burrata with fresh ground pepper, flaky sea salt and crushed red pepper. Finish the pizza with a drizzle of honey, hot honey or extra virgin olive oil, then slice into that crispy crust and break the creamy burrata cheese onto each slice as you go.

Toppings and Garnish (optional)

4 slices prosciutto

¼ cup (14 g) arugula

¼ cup (6 g) fresh basil leaves, chopped or cut with scissors

Fresh grated Parmigiano Reggiano

1 ball burrata, room temperature

Fresh ground pepper

Pinch of flaky sea salt

½ tbsp (3 g) crushed red pepper

1 tbsp (15 ml) honey or hot honey

Extra virgin olive oil, for drizzling

#BurrataSkilletPizza
#CheesePlease
#IndulgentEatsatHome

Winner Winner Chicken Dinner

No protein is as ubiquitous as chicken. It doesn't have the restrictions that beef or pork do in certain cultures, and it's more accessible, as almost every part of a chicken is readily found at markets and grocery stores around the world. It's also adaptable to every cooking style—you can bake, poach, steam, braise, smoke, grill, sous vide, deep-fry, panfry AND stir-fry it. While chicken can get a bad rep for being dry and unseasoned (looking at you, bland chicken breast for #gainz), it can also produce some of the most satisfying dishes that exist in the world.

Let's face it, there's almost nothing as ecstasy-inducing as your teeth hitting crunchy skin followed by the juices of tender chicken dripping into and around your mouth. If that description has you salivating, then you should try out my Giant Crispy Chicken Sandwich with Pickled Garlic–Tabasco® Mayo (page 88) that puts the endless fast food versions to shame, or my twice-fried Sweet and Spicy Korean Fried Chicken (page 94) for a saucier version. Then, there's the comfort of savory Filipino Chicken Adobo (page 91), which I've made using a non-traditional cooking technique to deliver crispy skin.

The final two recipes grind up chicken to transform it into two very distinct shapes: elongated footballs of Japanese-flavored chicken meatballs that get dipped into cured egg yolk (page 97) and a whole pizza made from chicken parm (page 101). No matter what you choose, you're sure to feel like a winner with these fun, shareable and super 'grammable dishes.

GIANT CRISPY CHICKEN SANDWICH
with Pickled Garlic–Tabasco® Mayo

It's no wonder the chicken emoji is a drumstick. It's the coveted piece with the perfect ratio of crunchy skin and tender, juicy meat. So why hasn't there been a chicken sandwich that includes the drumstick? Because despite the "chicken sandwich wars" where seemingly every fast-food chain and restaurant threw their version into the ring, the drumstick never made an appearance. That changes now though, thanks to my giant chicken sandwich.

While you can make it with just the chicken thigh or even chicken breast, if you prefer white meat, my BEHEMOTH of a chicken sandwich uses an entire boneless chicken leg with thigh and drumstick attached. You can find this cut at most supermarkets and even better, it's usually cheaper, as I suppose there are fewer uses for a connected boneless chicken thigh and drumstick. But the good news is that it produces the fullest, most moist mouthful of fried chicken between buns complete with homemade garlic dill pickles (page 223) and a smoked paprika Tabasco® mayo infused with the garlic from our pickles. They add a sharp acidic bite to perfectly complement our pickle-brined fried chicken.

Tip: Want to change up the flavors the second time you make this? Try swapping the pickled garlic for roasted garlic (page 224) and the Tabasco in the mayo for Sichuan Chili Crisp Oil (page 229) for a Sichuan-flavored fried chicken sammie or swap the mayo for ranch dressing and toss the chicken in either BBQ sauce or my Korean sweet and spicy glaze (page 94).

Makes 2 sandwiches

Chicken and Marinade

2 boneless whole chicken legs with thigh and drumstick attached, skin-on or skinless (substitute with chicken thighs or breasts)

½ cup (120 ml) pickle juice, store-bought or from homemade garlic dill pickles (page 223)

¼ cup (60 ml) buttermilk (substitute with regular milk with 1 tbsp [15 ml] white vinegar or lemon juice)

1 tbsp (15 ml) Tabasco sauce or other cayenne-based hot sauce like Crystal's® or Frank's RedHot®

1 egg, beaten

Canola or vegetable oil, for frying

Brine the chicken by adding it to a resealable bag along with the pickle juice, squeezing out as much air as possible so the chicken is fully submerged in the juice. Refrigerate for at least 4 hours or up to 12 hours—this will help tenderize the chicken and add flavor.

One hour before you plan to fry the chicken, remove it from the pickle brine and then transfer it to a bowl with the buttermilk and Tabasco. Let it marinate at room temperature for 1 hour, then add the beaten egg to the buttermilk and use tongs to fully coat the chicken in the buttermilk-egg mixture.

(continued)

Pickled Garlic–Tabasco Mayo

1–2 cloves pickled garlic
(page 223), grated or pressed
(substitute with roasted garlic
[page 224] or regular garlic)

4 tbsp (58 g) Kewpie mayo

1–2 tbsp (15–30 ml) Tabasco sauce
or other cayenne-based hot sauce
like Crystal's or Frank's RedHot
(substitute with Sichuan Chili
Crisp Oil [page 229])

½ tsp smoked paprika

Breading

¾ cup (94 g) self-rising flour, or
all-purpose flour with 1 tsp baking
powder

1 tbsp (10 g) cornstarch

1 tsp salt

1 tsp fresh ground pepper

1 tsp smoked paprika

1 tsp garlic powder

1 tsp onion powder

Sandwich Assembly

2 brioche burger buns or
potato rolls

10 garlic dill pickle chips
(page 223), plus more to taste

½ cup (35 g) shredded cabbage

Make the pickled garlic–Tabasco mayo while the chicken is marinating by whisking together the garlic, mayo, Tabasco and paprika until well combined.

Prepare the oil for frying by adding 1½ inches (4 cm) of oil to a Dutch oven or a wide, deep cast-iron skillet. Heat it over medium until it registers 350°F (180°C) on a thermometer. You can also test this by sticking a wooden chopstick into the oil—it's ready when bubbles form around the chopstick in the oil.

Meanwhile, whisk together the breading ingredients along with 2 tablespoons (30 ml) of the buttermilk-egg mixture in a shallow bowl, which will help make the breading extra crispy and craggy. Then, use tongs or your hands to add the chicken and fully coat it in the flour mixture, getting into all the crevices and pressing the flour into the chicken, shaking off any excess flour.

Fry the chicken for 7 to 9 minutes until golden brown and a thermometer registers 165°F (70°C) in the thickest part of the chicken, using tongs to flip over the chicken every couple of minutes. Depending on the size of your pan, you may need to do this in batches—make sure to reheat the oil to 350°F (180°C) before frying the second piece of chicken. Once cooked, set aside on a paper towel–lined plate to drain the excess oil.

Toast the buns while the chicken is frying, if desired.

Chicken sandwich ASSEMBLE! Spread the pickled garlic–Tobasco mayo on the toasted sides of the buns, then top the bottom bun with pickles. Place the fried chicken on top, then add shredded cabbage and the top bun. Sink your teeth into that juicy, ASMR-crispy chicken sandwich and enjoy!

#CrispyChickenSandwich #WinnerWinnerChickenDinner
#IndulgentEatsatHome

CRISPY OVEN-BRAISED FILIPINO CHICKEN ADOBO

Chicken adobo is the national dish of the Philippines. Every region and household has their own way of preparing this soy, vinegar and garlic braised chicken, from adding coconut milk or turmeric to removing the soy altogether. I have two versions of my mom's recipe that take a more traditional approach, but I created this recipe with crispy skin because, in my opinion, everything is better with a little crunch! Chicken adobo is typically made on the stove by braising everything in a covered pan, but it often results in chewy, less appetizing chicken skin.

Instead, we're going to maintain the crunch by panfrying the unmarinated skin until crispy, then braising the chicken in the adobo marinade in the oven. Does this go completely against the "laws" of chicken adobo? Probably, but in my biased opinion, it's forgiven since the intoxicating flavors of adobo remain unharmed! Whether this is your first taste of chicken adobo or your fiftieth, I hope you'll love the garlicky and deliciously pungent flavors that await.

Tip: Use Filipino brands of cane vinegar and soy sauce for the most authentic flavors. You can find Datu Puti® and Silver Swan® at Asian supermarkets or scan the QR code to shop on my website (plus watch how to make this dish). You can also skip the adobo all together and use this oven braising technique whenever you make chicken thighs. Try swapping the adobo ingredients with your favorite marinade and add veggies like potatoes or cauliflower to the pan to cook in the oven at the same time.

Makes 2 to 6 servings

6 bone-in, skin-on chicken thighs

¼ tsp salt

¾ cup (180 ml) cane vinegar (Datu Puti preferred), substitute with white or apple cider vinegar

½ cup (120 ml) soy sauce (Silver Swan preferred)

¾ cup (180 ml) water

6 cloves garlic, crushed

1 tbsp (10 g) whole peppercorns, crushed

2 bay leaves

1 tbsp (15 g) sugar

Cooked white rice, for serving

Preheat the oven to 350°F (180°C), making sure the oven rack is in the center position. You want to use a pan that is wide enough to fit all the pieces of chicken in a single layer, but not too wide where there would be big gaps between the chicken (I love using my Le Creuset® braiser for this). If your pan is not oven-safe, prepare a high-walled baking pan that will fit the chicken and set it aside for now—you will transfer the chicken and braising liquid from the pan to this baking pan later.

Season the chicken skin with salt, then add the chicken thighs to the pan skin side down. Cook over medium-high heat for 10 to 12 minutes until the skin is golden brown and crispy. About 6 minutes in, the chicken skin should release from the pan, making the chicken easy to move. Give the chicken skin a peek—if there are parts that are lighter than others, rearrange the chicken so the lighter parts are on the hotter parts of the pan. You won't need to add any oil since the chicken skin will render enough fat to fry itself.

Prepare the braising liquid while the chicken skin is panfrying. Grab a measuring cup and measure out the vinegar, then add the soy sauce and finally the water so you have 2 cups (480 ml) of liquid, then add the crushed garlic, peppercorns and bay leaves and set aside.

(continued)

CRISPY OVEN-BRAISED FILIPINO CHICKEN ADOBO (CONTINUED)

Flip over the chicken so the skin side is up and cook the other side for 1 minute, then set aside the half-cooked chicken on a large plate or tray, keeping the skin side up to not disrupt the crispy skin.

Add the braising liquid to the pan and mix in the sugar until dissolved. Bring to a boil over medium heat. Once boiling, add the chicken with the skin side up and bring to a boil again. If you are using a baking pan, carefully transfer the chicken back to the same plate or tray, pour the boiling hot adobo sauce into the baking pan and add the chicken to the pan with the skin side up. Be careful not to get the chicken skin wet.

Bake in the oven for 45 minutes until the liquid has reduced by about half and the chicken is fully cooked to tender, juicy perfection. Serve with white rice, spooning sauce onto the rice to enhance the chicken adobo flavors.

#CrispyChickenAdobo #WinnerWinnerChickenDinner #IndulgentEatsatHome

SWEET AND SPICY KOREAN FRIED CHICKEN

While most people picture Colonel Sanders holding a bucket from Kentucky when they hear KFC, my mind immediately goes to South Korea. I was first introduced to Korean Fried Chicken by way of the chain Bonchon, famous for their extra crispy, twice-fried soy-garlic wings that I often ate for dinner and as drunk food during my time at NYU and beyond. But during an overnight layover at Seoul's Incheon International Airport in 2019, we took a taxi into Incheon proper after learning about the famous sweet and spicy fried chicken at Sinpo International Market.

We managed to get to the stall 10 minutes before closing, which was enough time to feast our eyes on the MESMERIZING process of seeing giant bowls of fried chicken getting tossed in a glossy red sauce along with fresh chilis. It easily surpassed the soy-garlic wings that previously reigned supreme in my mind. While I frankly haven't figured out how to get my chicken to taste EXACTLY like theirs, it gets pretty darn close. I keep Bonchon's double-frying method for super crispy chicken but use easier-to-eat boneless chicken thighs cut into nuggets, instead. I hope you enjoy sinking your teeth into my version of Korean dakgangjeong!

Makes 2 to 4 servings

Korean Fried Chicken

1 lb (454 g) boneless, skinless chicken thighs

¼ cup (60 ml) milk

2 tbsp (30 ml) mirin

¼ tsp white pepper

¼ tsp ground ginger

¾ tsp salt

¾ cup (96 g) potato starch or cornstarch

Vegetable or canola oil, for frying

Scan this QR code to watch my video of the fried chicken at Incheon's Sinpo International Market, which has gained almost half a million views on Instagram, plus watch how to make my version.

In a non-reactive container, marinate the chicken in the milk, mirin, white pepper, ginger and salt for at least 30 minutes. Fill a medium bowl with the potato starch for later.

Prepare the oil by filling a deep medium-sized pot or Dutch oven with 1 inch (2.5 cm) of oil. Preheat the oil to 330°F (165°C) over medium-high heat.

Dredge the chicken in the potato starch or cornstarch, pressing the starch into the chicken to coat.

Once the oil is hot, fry half of the chicken for the first fry by carefully dropping the chicken into the oil. Cook for about 3 minutes until light golden brown—you are using this lower temperature fry to cook the inside of the chicken, so don't worry about getting color on the outside. Turn the pieces with a spider or slotted spoon occasionally, then drain it from the oil and transfer to a paper towel–lined plate or wire rack.

(continued)

SWEET AND SPICY KOREAN FRIED CHICKEN (CONTINUED)

Gochujang Honey Glaze

2 tbsp (33 g) gochujang

2 tbsp (30 ml) honey

2 tbsp (30 ml) rice vinegar

2 tbsp (30 ml) water

½ tbsp (7 ml) sesame oil

Garnishes

½ tbsp (4 g) sesame seeds

2 tbsp (18 g) crushed peanuts, optional

2 green chilis like Korean green chilis, Anaheim or other non-spicy green chili pepper, sliced diagonally into 1-inch (2.5-cm)-long pieces, optional

Bring the oil back up to temperature before adding the second batch of chicken—frying in two batches ensures the oil temperature doesn't drop too significantly.

Meanwhile, make the gochujang honey glaze by whisking together and simmering the gochujang, honey, vinegar, water and sesame oil in a wok or large saucepan over medium-low heat until you have a uniform, sticky glaze, 1 to 2 minutes. Remove from the heat while you finish frying the chicken.

Heat the oil to 375ºF (190ºC) for the second fry. Now that the chicken is cooked, we are only frying for color. Fry it in two batches until it's golden brown, 1 to 2 minutes, reheating the oil in between batches.

Add the fried chicken and garnishes to the glaze, then toss everything together. You'll be surprised at how crispy the chicken stays even in the glaze!

Serve immediately with an ice-cold beer for the true Korean experience. *Gunbae!* 🍗

#SweetandSpicyKFC #WinnerWinnerChickenDinner #IndulgentEatsatHome

TSUKUNE (CHICKEN MEATBALL YAKITORI)
with Egg Yolk Tare Dip

Dip it real good! Tsukune is my favorite type of yakitori (aka Japanese grilled skewers). Yakitori translates to "grilled chicken," as traditional yakitori restaurants in Japan showcase different parts of a chicken in their charcoal-grilled skewers, though it's since expanded to the grilled pork, beef and other items you'll find at izakaya or Japanese-style pubs around the world. This recipe is modeled after the incredibly popular tsukune at Yardbird HK, a cult-favorite izakaya in Hong Kong, along with the countless tsukune I've eaten in Japan.

What sets tsukune apart from meatballs in other cultures is that it's coated in tare, which can refer to ramen sauce (as it does for my earlier noodle recipes), but also means yakitori sauce. The sweetened soy-mirin-sake-based sauce gets brushed on as the chicken cooks to create a layer of umami-rich caramelization, which is then heightened when you dip the meatball into more tare mixed with an egg yolk. While it's easier to dip when it's on a stick, you can easily serve the tsukune without the skewers to eat with chopsticks. Either way, you're about to have a ball with this satisfying chicken dish.

Makes 6 skewers

Tare (Yakitori Sauce) and Egg Yolk Dip

½ cup (120 ml) sake

¼ cup (60 ml) mirin

¼ cup (60 ml) soy sauce

1 tbsp (17 g) brown sugar

3 stalks scallions, green tops only, chopped into thirds

1 slice ginger

2 egg yolks, pasteurized eggs (like Japanese eggs) recommended

Tsukune (Chicken Meatballs)

12 oz (340 g) ground chicken thighs

3 tbsp (20 g) panko bread crumbs

¼ onion, grated and squeezed dry

1 tsp mirin

1 tsp sake

½ tsp salt

½ tsp white pepper

In a small saucepan, make the tare by combining the sake, mirin, soy sauce, sugar, scallions and ginger. Bring to a boil over medium heat, then simmer over low heat for 10 minutes until the sauce has reduced by half. You can make this far in advance, just strain out the scallions and ginger, and it will keep in an airtight container in the fridge for up to 2 months.

Optional: Cure the egg yolks in tare—it will infuse a deep umami flavor into the eggs while keeping the yolk gooey so that it will stick to the tsukune better when you dip. Mix 2 tablespoons (30 ml) of tare with 2 tablespoons (30 ml) of water in a container and add the egg yolks in. Leave it in the refrigerator while you prepare the rest of the ingredients. **Otherwise,** you can just add the egg yolk right before serving.

In a large bowl, make the tsukune by combining the chicken, bread crumbs, onion, mirin, sake, salt and white pepper. You want to really mix and knead the ingredients to get it to bind and stick together, so use your hands to knead the filling for a couple of minutes until the mixture is sticky.

Divide the chicken mixture into six equal-sized meatballs—you can eyeball this by rolling them into balls and redistributing the meat until they're about even in size. If you have a scale, you should weigh out about 2 ounces (60 g) of meat per ball.

(continued)

TSUKUNE (CHICKEN MEATBALL YAKITORI) (CONTINUED)

Shape the tsukune. Take one ball of chicken, roll it into a short log and then squeeze the log between the palms of your hands as pictured. It will naturally begin to form a long football shape as you press and turn the meatball. Once all the footballs are shaped, put them back in the fridge for at least 30 minutes so they will hold their shape better. You can also make the meatballs the day before to really let them firm up.

Optional: Prepare the skewers, if you are using them. Soak the bamboo skewers for at least 30 minutes so they don't burn when you cook the tsukune—you can do this at the same time the tsukune is setting in the refrigerator. You can also cover the exposed skewers with aluminum foil for extra protection or use metal skewers, which are heatproof.

Prepare the dipping sauce by getting two small dipping bowls and putting 1½ tablespoons (22 ml) of tare into each one. Set aside the rest of the tare—you will use most of this to brush onto the tsukune. If the tare was in the fridge, you can heat up the tare before transferring it to the dipping bowls.

Optional: Make the skewers by pushing a skewer into the point of the meatball so it goes all the way through the center until the end of the skewer meets the end of the meatball. If the meatball gets misshapen, simply use your hands to reshape the meatball into a firm, compacted, football-shaped meatball on the skewer. Do this for all the tsukune.

(continued)

Optional Equipment
6 metal or bamboo skewers

Togarashi (Japanese chili pepper blend), for garnish (optional, but recommended)

Cook the tsukune until they are browned and caramelized on the outside and an instant-read thermometer reads 165°F (70°C) in the center of the thickest part of the meatball. There are three ways to cook the tsukune:

Option 1: Grill the tsukune. First make sure to clean and oil the grill grates. Preheat the grill for at least 5 minutes before using, then place the tsukune onto the grill and cook it without disturbing for 4 minutes, until well browned on one side, then carefully rotate and cook each side for 2 to 3 minutes, until well browned. Brush all over with tare and cook for another 15 to 30 seconds, rotating and brushing more tare as you go, then transfer to a serving platter.

Option 2: Bake the tsukune. Preheat the oven to broil on high or 450 to 500°F (230 to 260°C), depending on how high your oven can go. Use either a broiling pan or a baking tray with a wire rack that sits on top and brush it with canola or vegetable oil, then set the tsukune on top, leaving some space between each skewer. If using a broiling pan, they should fit right into the slots. Bake them on the center rack of the oven for 6 minutes, then flip and bake another 4 minutes. Brush all over with tare and bake another minute, then flip and brush all over again, baking for another minute. Watch them as they bake; if it looks like they might burn, reduce the heat in the oven. Once they are cooked, transfer to a serving platter.

Option 3: Air fry the tsukune. Preheat the air fryer to 400°F (200°C), then spray the bottom with canola oil. Place the tsukune in a single layer and air fry for 4 minutes, flip and air fry for another 3 minutes. Brush all over with tare and air fry for another minute, then flip and brush all over with tare again. Air fry for another minute or until cooked, then transfer to a serving platter.

Serve the tsukune by adding a cured or raw egg yolk to each dipping bowl, then serve alongside the tsukune. Dip the tsukune into the egg, mixing it into the tare so the sauce and yolk coat the meatball. I'd highly recommend sprinkling on some togarashi seasoning to add some heat and additional flavor!

#TsukunewithEggYolkTare #WinnerWinnerChickenDinner #IndulgentEatsatHome

CHICKEN PARM "PIZZA"

Say hello to the most protein-packed "pizza" around! NYC's Quality Italian took Instagram by storm when it introduced their Chicken Parmigiana for Two, shaping their delicious chicken parm into a giant thin patty cut into slices and served on a pizza pan. My own video of it went viral, gaining almost 70k likes. Since then, they've released new versions topped with everything from pancetta and eggs to shaved black truffles, but for the cookbook I wanted to keep it simple and show you how to make the original with marinara sauce, mozzarella and the namesake Parmigiano Reggiano. It's not that difficult to make as long as you have the time and the right pans, so give it a try for a fun and incredibly satisfying spin on pizza night.

Makes 2 to 4 servings

Ground Chicken Base

12 oz (340 g) boneless skinless chicken breasts, cubed, or lean ground chicken

1 tsp salt

1 tsp black pepper

1 tsp garlic powder

1 tsp onion powder

1 tsp paprika

½ tsp dried oregano

Canola or vegetable oil, for frying

Scan the QR code to watch Quality Italian's Chicken Parmigiana for Two get made.

Using a food processor, combine the cubed chicken, salt, pepper, garlic powder, onion powder, paprika and oregano to make the chicken base. It's important you use lean white chicken meat for this so that the "pizza" doesn't fall apart when you fry and bake it. Store-bought ground chicken can be quite fatty since it uses white and dark meat and sometimes skin, so if you don't have a food processor, try to request ground chicken made from chicken breasts from the butcher counter, and then just combine it well with the rest of the ingredients in a large bowl.

To form the ground chicken base, get a 9- or 10-inch (23- or 25-cm) cake pan or round baking dish and line it with a big layer of plastic wrap that's long enough to fully wrap the base on both sides. Add the seasoned ground chicken and use your hands to press it into the pan, forming an even, round layer that goes all the way to the edges. Wrap the excess plastic wrap on top and use a measuring cup to finish pressing it into a flat shape, then freeze it until it's completely frozen solid, 3 to 4 hours, or overnight.

Preheat the oil to 400°F (200°C) over medium heat in a wide skillet with high walls—you want to use enough oil to fully submerge the chicken parm and also make sure the skillet is wide enough for you to reach in with spatulas or tongs to pick up the chicken parm when it's done. Preheat the oven to broil or its highest temperature setting.

(continued)

Chicken Parm and Toppings

1 cup (125 g) flour

3 eggs, beaten

1 cup (108 g) panko bread crumbs (mix with ¼ cup [42 g] grated Parmesan)

1 cup (240 ml) Marinara Sauce (page 71) or Vodka Sauce (page 51)

1 cup (113 g) shredded low-moisture mozzarella

¼ cup (29 g) shredded fontina, substitute with mozzarella

½ cup (45 g) fresh grated Parmigiano Reggiano, plus more for serving

Fresh basil, for garnish

Crushed red pepper, for serving, optional

Garlic powder, for serving, optional

Now let's get BREADY to rumble! Prepare three shallow, separate dishes, one for the flour, another for the beaten eggs and a third for the bread crumbs mixed with Parmesan. The bowls should be large enough to fit the frozen chicken base. Unwrap the base and coat it all over with the flour, shaking off any excess. Then dip it into the eggs and finally, in the bread crumbs, pressing them into the chicken to fully and evenly coat it.

Fry the chicken parm base until golden brown all over, 4 to 6 minutes. Be careful when placing the disc into the hot oil—lower it gently with tongs so it doesn't splash. If needed, use tongs and a spatula to carefully flip over the base midway through for even browning on both sides. Once it's done, transfer the base to a paper towel–lined plate, blotting with paper towels to remove excess oil.

Add your toppings. First spread the sauce, then the shredded cheeses and finally the grated Parmigiano, spreading in an even layer and leaving a bit of a "crust" on the edge of the chicken parm "pizza."

Bake in the oven until the cheese is bubbly and has reached your preferred level of doneness—I like mine with lots of golden-brown spots. This will take 6 to 10 minutes depending on how golden you want the cheese. Remove from the oven and transfer to a serving plate.

Serve with torn fresh basil leaves and more Parmigiano, as desired. You can also put typical pizza seasonings like crushed red pepper and garlic powder on the side. Cut into slices and watch that cheese-pull!

#ChickenParmPizza #WinnerWinnerChickenDinner #IndulgentEatsatHome

Meat Sweats

Apologies to any vegetarians out there, but there is simply no greater satisfaction than biting into a juicy, tender, perfectly cooked piece of meat. Truthfully, I weigh the ethical and environmental weight of eating meat every day. We cannot dismiss the impact it has on our planet, and I encourage everyone who DOES love meat to consider adopting my approach—cut down on your daily meat consumption and save it for the REALLY GOOD STUFF. And every recipe in this section definitely falls into that category. This means skipping the cheap grocery store beef on a weeknight and waiting for a special occasion to smash the juiciest burgers (page 106), slow cook a giant pot of meat for some of the best tacos on the planet (page 113) or revel in the ultimate indulgence of a deep-fried Wagyu beef sandwich (page 125). That said, you could easily apply these techniques to plant-based meat like Impossible™ (which I've actually had great success in using to make Bolognese!), so I encourage you to make swaps where it makes sense.

You may notice that most of these meaty dishes aren't solely meat focused. There's meat as a sandwich filling, meat as a taco filling, meat as a dip—and that's on purpose. You can make the entire recipe as I've laid it out, or just make the meat and repurpose it as you see fit. Go ahead and turn my smashed burgers (page 106) into lettuce wraps with your own burger sauce. Make the *lechon kawali* that is nestled in my pork belly *sisig* recipe (page 111) and eat it in a steamed bao. Slow cook the meaty Bolognese sauce (page 119) to enjoy in a lasagna or with zucchini noodles instead of with the cheesy garlic bombs prescribed. That's the beauty of meat—it's so incredibly versatile that it can turn everything from plain veggies to elaborate sandwiches into the most satisfying dishes you've ever had.

EAST MEETS WEST COAST DOUBLE SMASHED BURGERS

For me, smashed burgers make the BEST burgers, but there's also science to back it up: Smashing maximizes the contact points between the meat and the hot pan, increasing the beef's Maillard reaction to develop a dark crust and, in turn, more umami. My ideal form of a burger pulls from some of my favorite Insta-famous burgers from coast to coast with added Asian-inspired flair (hence the name, get it?). It's got smashed patties and Martin's® Potato Rolls like the East Coast favorite Shake Shack®, griddled onions and chopped chilis like West Coast institution In-N-Out®, a Korean gochujang-based sauce like NYC's Pizza Loves Emily, house-made pickles like NYC's Pig Beach and Thai-Vietnamese–style fried shallots to add a bit of crunch.

I've also used the "Oklahoma Onion" technique that I learned from my friend Michael Puma of Gotham Burger Social Club, where you smash very thinly sliced onions right into the patty to produce a caramelized onion–like griddled onion. And finally, it has both melty cheese AND a crispy cheese skirt, a technique I learned from my fellow Filipino-American chef Alvin Cailan who hosts The Burger Show. *It's beefy, juicy, cheesy, savory, spicy, crispy, acidic and just all-around drool-worthy—everything you want a burger to be.*

Makes 2 double-patty burgers

Roasted Garlic Gochujang Mayo

1 tsp white sesame seeds, optional

6 cloves roasted garlic (page 224)

6 tbsp (86 g) Kewpie mayo

1–2 tbsp (17–34 g) gochujang

1 tsp rice vinegar

Scan the QR code to watch how to smash these burgers.

Toast the sesame seeds, if you're using them. It's a tiny bit of extra work, but I'd recommend including it, as the nutty flavor really complements the roasted garlic and gochujang to make this irresistible. To toast them, heat a saucepan over medium-high heat, then toss the sesame seeds in the pan until they are golden brown all over. Grind the toasted sesame seeds using a mortar and pestle or spice grinder, or let them cool and then pound them into a powder with a rolling pin in a resealable bag.

Make the roasted garlic gochujang mayo. Blend the sesame powder along with the garlic, mayo, gochujang and vinegar until smooth. Set aside or make ahead and store in the refrigerator in an airtight container for up to 5 days ahead of time.

(continued)

Smashed Burgers

1 tbsp (15 ml) vegetable or canola oil

1 tbsp (14 g) butter, melted

2 Martin's potato rolls, substitute with brioche, plain or sesame seeded burger bun

8 oz (226 g) fresh ground beef chuck (Wagyu preferred), rolled into 2 oz (57 g) balls

¼ medium onion, very thinly sliced (substitute with 4 tbsp [72 g] caramelized onions for extra sweetness [page 220]), optional

Salt, to taste

Preheat a cast-iron skillet or flat griddle pan over medium-high heat and brush with oil.

Toast the buns in the meantime by melting the butter in a nonstick skillet over medium heat, spreading the butter in a thin even layer, then rub the cut ends of the buns into the pan so they're evenly coated in butter. Raise the heat to medium-high and let them sit on the skillet until they are golden brown, 1 to 2 minutes. While you prepare the patties, stick the toasted buns into an airtight container or resealable bag, leaving a small opening for some steam to escape. This will keep them warm and steam the rest of the bun just slightly so they're soft and pillowy, a similar effect to wrapping up a burger bun in foil.

LET'S SMASH! Place the balls of burger meat on the preheated cast-iron skillet or griddle with 2 to 3 inches (5 to 8 cm) of space between each ball. You may have to do this one at a time or in batches depending on the size of your pan. (Optional: Top each ball with a quarter of the thinly sliced onions.) Then use a burger smasher (my weapon of choice), a thin flat spatula (with no slits!), a small frying pan or a sturdy flat-bottomed cereal bowl to smash each ball, using all your force to create a thin patty about 4 inches (10 cm) in diameter. If you're using a spatula, use a wooden spoon with your other hand to press on the blade of the spatula to help get the patty flatter. If you're using a pan or bowl, you may want to lay a piece of parchment paper on top of the ball of beef before smashing so it doesn't stick. Try to make the edges very thin—this will help them really caramelize and crisp. Season with salt and let it cook without touching it for 1½ to 2 minutes until a crust has developed.

Meanwhile, make the crispy cheese layer. Sprinkle the shredded cheddar cheese into two circles in the same nonstick pan you used to toast the buns, and heat it over medium, leaving it in the pan so it melts, bubbles and eventually starts to crisp up while your burger patties cook.

Flip over the patties, using a bench scraper and/or a thin spatula to scrape up the crispy edges before flipping over. Top two of the patties with the slices of American cheese, then cover and cook for 1 to 2 minutes until the cheese has started to melt on the edges. To aid in the cheese melting, you can add a few drops of water to the outside edge of the pan before you cover it. Meanwhile, the other two patties only need to cook for a minute before you transfer each one onto a circle of crispy cheese so they meld together. Top the crispy cheese patty with the melted cheese patty.

Smashed burgers, ASSEMBLE! Spread the mayo onto the toasted side of both the top and bottom buns, then line the bottom bun with pickles. Add the double stack of burger patties with a crispy cheese skirt base, then top with caramelized onions (if using), jalapeños, fried shallots and finally the top bun. Be very quick with any photos so you can eat this while it's fresh off the griddle for maximum indulgence.

#EastMeetsWestCoastBurger #MeatSweats
#IndulgentEatsatHome

Burger Toppings

½ cup (113 g) shredded cheddar cheese

2 slices sharp American cheese (substitute with cheddar cheese but it's better with American!)

Garlic Dill Pickles, to taste (page 223, or store-bought)

4 tbsp (56 g) pickled jalapeños, chopped (page 223, or store-bought)

2 tbsp (12 g) fried shallots (find online or at any Asian supermarket)

FILIPINO SIZZLING PORK BELLY SISIG

The Philippines might be the most pork-obsessed country in the world. We celebrate special occasions with trays of crispy fried pork belly (lechon kawali) or go big with a whole roasted pig (lechon) that the late great Anthony Bourdain once dubbed the best pig in the world. We eat it daily for breakfast (page 19), as a snack in spring rolls (lumpia), and even add it to most of our vegetable dishes to the dismay of vegetarians everywhere. We also use every part of the pig, so nothing goes to waste, and that's where sizzling sisig comes in.

This addictive, soy and citrus-flavored pork dish comes on a sizzling platter topped with an egg. It is so delicious that non-Filipinos are shocked to learn that what they've just eaten is typically the pig's face, ears and snout, though I'm using more readily available pork belly in this recipe instead. It gets fried to crispy lechon kawali perfection, though there are shortcuts if you don't want to deep-fry. No matter which route you take, you're in for an ASMR-worthy, sizzling plate of goodness that's made for drinking or soaking up a hangover.

Makes 3 to 6 servings

Pork Belly/Lechon Kawali (substitute with leftover pork, roasted/fried chicken, cooked squid or tuna)

1 lb (454 g) pork belly, with skin on if deep-frying, cut into 1-inch (2.5-cm) pieces

4 dried bay leaves

6 cloves garlic, crushed

2 tbsp (30 ml) white vinegar

1 tbsp (10 g) whole black peppercorns

1 tbsp (18 g) salt

Canola or vegetable oil, for frying, optional

Decide which protein you are using in your sisig. This recipe includes directions for making lechon kawali, which you can enjoy on its own or chop up to use for your sisig—if going this route, make sure you are using pork belly with the skin on. If you'd prefer not to do any deep-frying, use skinless pork belly and follow the instructions for cooking the pork, but skip the deep-frying step—you will add crushed chicharron later to substitute for the crispy skin. You can also make sisig using whatever cooked protein you have on hand—just skip ahead to the "Chop your chosen protein" step and adjust the seasonings depending on whether the protein was already seasoned.

Fill a pot with the pork belly, bay leaves, garlic, white vinegar, peppercorns, salt and enough water to cover everything. Heat it over medium heat until it comes to a boil, then lower the heat and cover, letting it simmer for 1 hour. This will help the meat stay tender but not fall apart, and the pig skin will be soft and gelatinous so it will fry up crispy. Drain the meat and set aside. If you are making lechon kawali, let it cool to room temperature before storing in the refrigerator uncovered overnight so the moisture dries out. If storing for longer, then transfer it into an airtight container after it has dried; it will keep for another 2 to 3 days.

If making lechon kawali, heat a 2-inch (5-cm) layer of oil in a Dutch oven or high-walled pot over medium heat until it reaches 375°F (190°C). Get a splatter screen or large skillet lid ready as there will likely be some splatter, then add the cooked pork belly and fry until golden brown and crispy, 3 to 5 minutes. Use a spider or tongs to transfer to a wire rack or paper towel–lined plate to drain excess oil.

(continued)

FILIPINO SIZZLING PORK BELLY SISIG (CONTINUED)

Sisig

1 tbsp (14 g) butter (substitute with canola oil or vegetable oil)

½ medium yellow onion, chopped (substitute with red onion)

2 cloves garlic, minced

1–2 green chilis, stemmed, seeded and chopped

1½ tbsp (22 ml) soy sauce

1 tbsp (15 ml) cane or white vinegar

Juice from 4 calamansi, ½ lemon or ½ lime

Fresh ground pepper

Garnish

½ medium red onion, chopped

1–2 Thai bird's eye chilis, stemmed and seeded, if desired, then chopped

¼ cup (8 g) chicharrón (fried pork rinds), crushed, optional

3 tbsp (43 g) Kewpie mayo, optional

1–2 eggs

Chopped scallions

Calamansi halves or lemon/lime wedges

Spiced Vinegar

2–4 tbsp (30–60 ml) cane or white vinegar

1–2 cloves garlic, crushed

½–1 chopped Thai bird's eye chili

Fresh ground pepper

Cooked white rice or Garlic Rice (page 21), for serving

Chop your chosen protein into very small pieces, ¼ to ½ inch (6 mm to 1.3 cm) in size and set aside.

Make the sisig by heating the butter or oil in a skillet over medium heat. Add the onion and cook while stirring until softened, 6 to 8 minutes. While the onion is cooking, preheat a cast-iron platter or cast-iron skillet over medium-high to serve the sisig—this is what makes it sizzle! Once the onion is soft, add the garlic and chopped chilis and cook for another minute until aromatic. Add your chosen protein, then mix with the soy sauce, vinegar, citrus juice and fresh ground pepper to taste until heated through and fully combined.

Transfer the sisig to the cast-iron pan, then remove it from the heat. Mix in half the red onion, then distribute the remaining red onion, bird's eye chili and crushed chicharrón (if using) over the top. Drizzle the Kewpie mayo (if using) in a zigzag pattern over the sisig and make a well in the center for you to drop the egg(s) into. Garnish with chopped scallions and place the calamansi, lemon or lime wedges between the egg and the edge of the pan so they're easy to grab.

Serve immediately so the pan is still sizzling. Squeeze the citrus over the top, then use a spoon to break the egg and mix everything together until well combined. Serve with white rice or garlic rice or try it as a taco filling, along with the spiced vinegar, which you can make by simply combining the vinegar, garlic, bird's eye chili and pepper—it will add another pop of acidity to balance out this rich, meaty dish.

#SizzlingSisig #MeatSweats #IndulgentEatsatHome

BIRRIA AND BONE MARROW QUESOTACOS AND CRUNCHWRAPS

Who can resist juicy, meat-filled tacos dripping with rich beef consomé? Birria tacos became Insta-famous in recent years thanks to a number of taco trucks in Los Angeles, including Tacos y Birria La Unica where I first tried this dish, but for the cookbook I had to take it up a notch by adding whole roasted bone marrow! It's photogenic on its own, but also provides an extra luscious texture and satisfying beefy flavor.

Birria itself refers to the braised meat stew from Mexico, with different versions at every single birreria across regions like Jalisco, Tijuana and beyond. It can be made with beef, lamb, oxtail and/or goat and is traditionally served with warm tortillas, though these days it's found as burritos and even ramen. This birria de res (beef birria) is best eaten as a quesotaco, with the juicy meat and bone marrow pressed between melty cheese and fresh corn tortillas crisped up in the red oil that develops in the birria. Or try making a Taco Bell®–inspired Crunchwrap Supreme® with more accessible flour tortillas plus tortilla chips to create the crunch. Regardless of which vehicle you choose, make sure to get your napkins ready—you're in for a treat.

Makes 20 to 30 quesotacos or crunchwraps

Birria de Res

2 lbs (907 g) boneless beef chuck, cut into 2-inch (5-cm) cubes

1 lb (454 g) oxtail or bone-in short rib, cut into 2-inch (5-cm) cubes, if necessary

1 tbsp (18 g) salt

4 tbsp (60 ml) canola oil

6 cups (1.4 L) water

Adobo

6 dried guajillo peppers, de-stemmed and seeds removed

4 dried ancho peppers, de-stemmed and seeds removed

4 dried chipotle peppers, de-stemmed and seeds removed (feel free to play around with the ratios and types of dried chiles used)

1 white onion, quartered

10 cloves garlic, peeled

1 (2-inch [5-cm]) piece ginger, peeled and roughly chopped

2 bay leaves

You can make the birria de res up to 3 days or 3 months ahead of when you will serve the tacos or crunchwraps for easier prep—storing the meat with the consomé also infuses the flavors into the beef even more. Follow my instructions for storing the components in the fridge or freezer.

Season the beef generously all over with salt and let it come to room temperature for at least 30 minutes. Even better, season the beef with salt the night before and put it back in the refrigerator so the salt can permeate the beef, then take it out at least 30 minutes before cooking.

Make the adobo while the meat comes to room temperature. First, toast the dried chile peppers. Heat them in a skillet over medium-high for 1 to 2 minutes until they are aromatic. This really brings out the flavor and aromas in the skins. Then add the toasted chile peppers, along with the onion, garlic, ginger and bay leaves to a large saucepan and fill it with water until the ingredients are mostly submerged, 5 to 6 cups (1.2 to 1.4 L). Bring to a boil over medium-high, then cook uncovered over medium heat for 10 minutes while stirring occasionally until the chiles are softened. Drain the chile mixture, discarding the cooking liquid and bay leaves.

(continued)

¼ cup (60 ml) white vinegar

1 large tomato or 2 small tomatoes, halved (substitute with ½ cup [120 g] canned crushed tomatoes)

½ tsp ground cumin

½ tsp ground cinnamon

1½ tsp (2 g) dried oregano, Mexican preferred

½ tsp dried thyme

2 cups (480 ml) chicken or beef stock

Roasted Bone Marrow (optional)

3–4 pieces bone marrow at least 6 inches (15 cm) long, cut in half lengthwise by the butcher

½ tsp flaky sea salt

In a blender or food processor, combine the adobo ingredients with the vinegar, tomato, cumin, cinnamon, oregano, thyme and stock until smooth. Don't worry if there are some bits of spices as you can strain them out later. Set aside.

Brown the meat by heating a Dutch oven or stockpot over medium heat, then add the oil and sear the meat on all sides when the oil is shimmering. You may have to do this in two batches depending on how wide your Dutch oven is. Return all the seared meat to the pot.

Add the adobo and water to the pot so the meat is fully submerged, then bring to a boil over medium heat uncovered, stirring occasionally. In the meantime, preheat the oven to 300°F (150°C) if your pan is oven-safe. I prefer making the birria in the oven since it's more hands-off, but I'll explain how you can also make this on the stove if you don't have an oven-safe pot.

Once the adobo mixture is boiling, cover the pot. If you are making this in the oven, transfer it to your preheated oven and cook for 3 hours until the beef is easy to shred with two forks. If you are cooking on the stovetop, lower the heat to medium-low and simmer for 3 hours until the beef is easy to shred.

Transfer the cooked beef from the consomé to a large bowl. Discard any bones, pulling the meat off the bone, then shred all the beef with two forks and mix together. You can also do this in a stand mixer with the paddle attachment on low speed after you've removed the bones.

Strain the consomé using a fine mesh strainer to remove any floating bits of adobo ingredients. If making the birria ahead of time, let the meat and consomé come to room temperature before storing them together in an airtight container.

Optional: Roast the bone marrow. Preheat the oven to 450°F (230°C). Sprinkle the tops of the bone marrow with sea salt, then roast in the center rack of the oven for 20 to 25 minutes until the bones are golden brown and the bone marrow looks golden and gelatinous. Turn off the oven and leave it to cool inside.

(continued)

Quesotacos and Crunchwraps

20–30 (4–5-inch [10–13-cm]) corn tortillas, as needed, the fresher the better (substitute with 8-inch [20-cm] or larger flour tortillas to make crunchwraps)

2–4 cups (226–450 g) shredded Oaxaca cheese or mozzarella mixed with Monterey Jack or other Mexican cheese blend

1 large onion, chopped

1–2 bunches cilantro, chopped

Corn tortillas to be deep fried, tostadas or tortilla chips for crunchwrap, optional

Meanwhile, skim off the red oil sitting on top of the consomé—this is your birria oil and you will need it to fry the tortillas. If you made the birria ahead of time, you can easily scrape the oil off the top of the chilled consomé before reheating each component separately. Set it aside in a small bowl or container.

Simmer the remaining consomé over medium heat until it has reduced by half, about 15 minutes. If you made the birria ahead of time, strain the beef out of the consomé and set aside before simmering the consomé until it has reduced by half. It should be ready around the same time as the bone marrow. Divide the consomé into small bowls for each person to dip into.

Make the quesotacos. Dip a corn tortilla in the birria oil then cook oil side down in a large skillet over medium heat, up to four tacos at a time. Top with shredded cheese all over, letting the cheese go all the way to the edges to develop a crispy cheese edge, then add chopped birria beef to one side of the taco. Spoon the chopped onion and cilantro on top of the beef, as well as a small spoonful of bone marrow right out of the bone (if using). Once the cheese has started to melt, use a spatula (or two) to fold over the taco, then press down and flatten the taco so the melted cheese bonds with the fillings. Continue cooking, flipping as needed, until the taco is crispy all over (this will also reheat the beef if you made it ahead of time), repeating this process until you use all the beef. You can also store leftover birria in the fridge for up to 3 days or in the freezer for up to 3 months.

Make the crunchwraps. First, you'll need to prepare the crunchy element. You can either deep-fry whole corn tortillas in 325°F (160°C) oil until golden and crispy to make your own tostadas, or use store-bought tostadas or simply tortilla chips.

When you're ready to make the crunchwrap, cut the flour tortilla halfway down the middle. Spread 1 to 2 tablespoons (15 to 30 ml) of birria oil across the bottom of a large skillet over medium heat, placing the flour tortilla onto the oil and moving it around to evenly coat with oil, then position the tortilla so the cut in the tortilla is closest to you.

In the first quadrant to the left of the cut, place the tostada or tortilla chips (you will need to break the tostada to fit). You can also add some sliced or smashed avocado seasoned with salt, if desired, though I personally prefer my birria without it.

In the second quadrant above that, add the onion and cilantro plus pickled red onions and bone marrow (if using).

In the third quadrant going clockwise, add the birria meat in an even layer—remember that you will be flipping each quadrant onto the other, so try not to put too much filling or everything will spill out.

In the final quadrant to the right of the cut, add the cheese. Now use a spatula and your hands to flip the entire wrap onto itself—flip the first tostada quadrant onto the onions, then flip that onto the beef and finally flip the entire thing onto the cheese, using the melting cheese to act as a seal. Continue cooking, flipping as needed, until the crunchwrap is crispy all over, repeating this process until you use all the beef.

Serve the quesotacos and crunchwraps with consomé, scooping leftover marrow into the consomé for extra flavor or sticking the whole bone into the bowl. Give the tacos a squeeze of lime all over, adding pickled red onions and hot sauce as desired, before dipping into the consomé and enjoying this gift from the taco gods.

#BirriaQuesotacos #MeatSweats #IndulgentEatsatHome

Garnishes

Avocado, optional

Pickled red onions (page 223)

Lime wedges

Habanero hot sauce (I love El Yucateco® with these)

BOLOGNESE

with Cheesy Garlic Bombs

If you're looking for love, look no further than Bolognese. Cooked low and slow for hours, you can taste the time and effort that goes into the sauce. Bolognese (pronounced bo-loan-yay-zay) is so much more than meat sauce, though if you get the ingredients wrong, an Italian person will likely tell you that it IS meat sauce and NOT Bolognese. That's because it originates from Bologna, Italy, where it's simply referred to as ragù and has specific ingredients and directions to qualify it as Bolognese (much like carbonara). With a lot of quick meat sauces that claim to be Bolognese, it's understandable why there's so much protection over the sauce.

So, it's with that note that I apologize to all the Italians for pairing this treasured sauce with something as American as these cheesy garlic bombs 😋. You can easily have the Bolognese with pasta, but this crowd-pleasing dish is a fun break from tradition. We're keeping things simple by using store-bought pizza dough, biscuit dough or crescent rolls so you can assemble the mozzarella-stuffed garlic bombs without the need to make dough from scratch.

Tip: *Always save your Parmigiano rinds! You can throw them into soups and sauces, like this Bolognese, to add extra umami.*

Makes 6 to 12 servings of Bolognese and 30 cheesy garlic bombs

My Version of Bolognese

1 medium onion, finely chopped

1 large celery stalk, finely chopped

1 small carrot, peeled and finely chopped

3 tbsp (45 ml) extra virgin olive oil

1 tbsp (14 g) butter

8 oz (226 g) ground beef, at least 20% fat, chuck preferred (substitute with Impossible meat)

8 oz (226 g) ground pork (substitute with ground beef or Impossible meat)

3 oz (85 g) pancetta, finely chopped, optional

Pinch of salt

2 cloves garlic, minced, optional as it's not traditional

1 cup (240 ml) dry white wine or red wine (I usually just use a cup of whatever wine I'm drinking while cooking, though white wine is traditional)

Let's make the Bolognese sauce. We're building layers of flavor, so while it might seem like a lot of steps, each one will bring more depth and deliciousness to the sauce—it's a good time to get a podcast or movie you love playing in the background.

Cook the soffritto, the Italian term for onion, celery and carrot that's commonly known as *mirepoix* or the "holy trinity." For ease in prep, you can pulse the roughly chopped vegetables in the food processor until finely chopped, but be careful not to over process it into a paste. Heat the olive oil and butter over medium heat in a Dutch oven or large pot, then add the soffritto and stir to coat all the vegetables in fat. Cook until the onion is translucent, and the carrot and celery are soft, while stirring occasionally, 5 to 7 minutes.

Add the ground meat and pancetta (if using) and season with a pinch of salt, then use a wooden spoon to break up the meat and combine it with the soffritto. Cook until well browned all over while breaking up the meat and stirring occasionally, 10 to 12 minutes. If using, add the garlic and cook for another minute until aromatic.

Add the wine and scrape up any bits that might be stuck to the bottom of the pot. Simmer over medium until the wine is absorbed into the meat mixture while continuing to break up the meat into tiny bits, 8 to 10 minutes.

(continued)

BOLOGNESE (CONTINUED)

1 cup (240 ml) whole milk

⅛ tsp ground nutmeg

2 tbsp (34 g) tomato paste (plus 3 more tbsp [51 g] if omitting crushed tomatoes to keep it more traditional)

1 bay leaf

2 cups (480 ml) low-sodium beef, chicken or vegetable broth, plus more as needed

14.5 oz (406 g) whole peeled San Marzano or Italian plum tomatoes, hand crushed, optional

1 Parmigiano cheese rind, optional

Cheesy Garlic Bombs

2 tbsp (30 ml) olive oil, divided

2 cans (16–22 oz [448–616 g]) ready-made pizza dough, biscuit dough or crescent rolls, cut into 30 squares

8 oz (226 g) low-moisture mozzarella, cut into 30 cubes

6 tbsp (84 g) butter, melted

6 cloves garlic, minced

½ cup (12 g) fresh Italian or flat-leaf parsley, chopped

Fresh grated Parmigiano, as desired

Add the milk and nutmeg and continue to simmer while stirring occasionally until the milk has fully evaporated, another 8 to 10 minutes.

Mix in the tomato paste (including the extra tomato paste if you are omitting the crushed tomatoes) and cook until the color has darkened, 5 to 7 minutes.

Add the bay leaf and broth, along with the crushed tomatoes and Parmigiano rind, if using. Let it come to a simmer, then reduce the heat to low.

Cook uncovered for 3 hours or more, the longer the better! Stir it occasionally, and if the mixture looks like it's drying out, add ½ cup (120 ml) of broth or water as you go. The meat will break down in the liquid into a luxurious sauce as it simmers, so it's worth putting in the time and work. If there's any sauce you aren't using right away, set it aside to come to room temperature before transferring it to an airtight container to store in the fridge for 3 to 5 days or in the freezer for up to 3 months.

Prepare the cheesy garlic bombs during the last 30 to 45 minutes of cooking the Bolognese. Preheat the oven to 400°F (200°C), then prepare a cast-iron skillet or other 10-inch (25-cm) or wider round pan by coating it with 1 tablespoon (15 ml) of olive oil. Then find an oven-safe ramekin or bowl to put in the center of the pan—you'll use this to shape the garlic bombs and fill the space with Bolognese later.

Roll out your chosen dough; press and seal together the seams if you are using crescent roll dough. You want to roll it out wide/long enough so that you can cut each roll into 15 squares, three wide and five long, so you will have 30 squares in total.

Place a cube of mozzarella in the center of each square, then wrap the dough around and press to seal all the edges.

Make the garlic butter by combining the remaining tablespoon (15 ml) of olive oil, melted butter, minced garlic and chopped parsley in a small bowl. Dip each dough ball in the garlic butter before placing it in the skillet around the ramekin/bowl for the sauce; make two layers of dough balls in the pan. Pour any remaining garlic butter all over the dough balls.

Bake the cheesy garlic bombs on the center rack of the oven for 15 to 25 minutes until golden brown on top. Let them set and cool for a few minutes, then you can either fill the ramekin with Bolognese sauce or carefully remove the ramekin from the center and fill the void with sauce.

Freshly grate the Parmigiano on top, right in front of your guests, then allow them to pull apart the ring of cheesy garlic bombs, ripping them to reveal the cheese-pull in the center and spooning on the Bolognese to enjoy altogether.

#BolognesewithCheesyGarlicBombs #MeatSweats
#IndulgentEatsatHome

CUBAN SANDWICH
with Mojo Roast Pork

Chef is my all-time favorite food movie. I love the feel-good story and how it highlights three incredible food cities in the U.S. The only downside is that it WILL leave you hungry, especially for the Cuban sandwiches, or Cubanos, in the film, but thankfully we can all make them at home with this recipe! It's the ultimate celebration of pork in a sandwich, featuring both marinated roast pork and sliced ham pressed between toasted Cuban bread with melted Swiss cheese, pickles and yellow mustard. Cubanos are the product of immigration, originating from the Cuban communities in South Florida with a deep rivalry between Miami and Tampa (where genoa salami is added).

I've never been to Tampa, but I have tried five different Cubanos throughout my trips to Miami, including my favorite from Sanguich de Miami that this recipe is based on. It's layered with juicy roast pork marinated in mojo, a Cuban marinade ripe with tangy, garlicky flavors that can be used on practically any protein. It's traditionally made with sour oranges native to Florida, so instead we're using orange and lime to create the sourness that plays with the garlic, herbs and spices for a rich, vibrantly flavored pork.

Tip: *Have leftover mojo pork? Try making a plate of mojo pork, rice, beans and tostones (crispy fried plantains) that you can dip into reserved mojo, or use it as the protein in a bunch of my other recipes: quesotacos and crunchwraps, breakfast sandwiches, mac and cheese, fried rice or empanadas. Just adjust the other ingredients and seasonings to account for the spices in the mojo pork.*

Makes 1 Cuban sandwich and pork for 6 to 8 sandwiches

Mojo Roast Pork

½ cup (120 ml) orange juice

¼ cup (60 ml) lime juice

1 tbsp (3 g) fresh oregano leaves, about 1 sprig, or ½ tbsp (2 g) dried oregano

1 cup (16 g) loosely packed cilantro, about 2 bunches, hard stems removed

¼ cup (4 g) mint

6 cloves garlic

½ cup (120 ml) olive oil

1 tsp fresh ground pepper

1 tsp salt, more to taste

2.2 lbs (1 kg) pork shoulder or pork butt

Make the mojo. Blend the orange juice, lime juice, oregano, cilantro, mint, garlic, olive oil and pepper until smooth. Reserve ½ cup (120 ml) of mojo and season with salt to taste. Store in an airtight container in the fridge to use to add more flavor to your Cubano later or as a sauce for the pork, tostones, fries, rice . . . anything.

Marinate the pork. First blend in 1 teaspoon of salt into the remaining mojo, then, using a resealable bag or large container, cover the pork shoulder all over, turning it and rubbing the marinade into the crevices. Let it marinate for at least 2 hours or overnight—if you're using a resealable bag, you may want to lay the bag inside of a container or on a plate in case of leakage. Remove the pork from the refrigerator 1 hour before you plan to roast it and transfer it out of the marinade and into a roasting pan. If there's any marinade left, save it—you will baste it onto the pork while it's roasting for extra flavaaa.

(continued)

Cuban Sandwich (makes 1 sandwich, multiply as needed)

1 piece Cuban bread or 1 ciabatta bun

1 tbsp (14 g) butter, softened or melted

1 tbsp (15 ml) mojo, optional

2–4 slices Swiss cheese (substitute with Emmental)

3–6 slices Garlic Dill Pickles (page 223), plus a few spears for garnish

1 tbsp (16 g) yellow mustard

2–4 slices Black Forest ham or other thinly sliced deli ham

4–6 oz (113–170 g) mojo roast pork, sliced

Roast the pork. Preheat the oven to 275°F (135°C), then bake the pork with the fat cap up in a roasting pan or baking pan for 2½ hours, basting or brushing the pork with any leftover marinade and pan juices occasionally. Raise the heat to 350°F (180°C), which will help develop a darker brown crust. Baste the pork again and continue roasting for an additional 30 minutes to an hour or until the pork reaches an internal temperature of 160°F (70°C), and it's tender enough that you can pull off a piece from the side with a fork. If you are using a larger cut of pork, you will need to add at least 30 minutes of roasting time per pound (454 g). It will take some time, but trust me—the result of juicy, tender pork is worth it! Let the pork rest for 10 to 15 minutes on a cutting board before you slice it. Make sure to slice against the grain—you can either slice it super thinly, to the same width as the ham, or in thicker slices based on personal preference. Slicing it thinner will make it a bit easier to bite into.

Prepare the Cubanos. Slice the bread in half lengthwise and coat the outside of the bread with butter before layering the rest of the ingredients. First, brush the inside of the top of the bread with mojo, if desired, then top it with the cheese and pickles. Drizzle the inside of the bottom with the mustard, then top it with the ham and then pork, then put the halves together to make your sandwich. Feel free to pile on the toppings to make it as meaty as you'd like!

Press and toast the Cubanos. You want to flatten the sandwiches to about a third of their size, leaving them golden brown and crispy on the outside with the cheese nice and melty. If you have a panini or sandwich press, you can heat that up and then press the sandwiches. You can also use two cast-iron skillets, a griddle and a Dutch oven or two regular skillets plus a heavy weight like a brick wrapped in foil as you want something heavy on top. Heat up both pans over medium heat, then once they're hot, place the sandwiches inside the skillet or griddle, top it with foil, then use force to press the second heated pan down onto the sandwich to act as a manual panini press. This is a good time to cue Salt-N-Pepa's "Push It"—you really want to push down and smush those layers together! Reheat the top skillet or flip the sandwich over as necessary to evenly toast both sides.

Serve while it's hot, slicing in half or diagonally with a side of mojo for dipping, potato chips and a pickle.

#CubanSandwich #MeatSweats #IndulgentEatsatHome

WAGYU KATSU SANDO

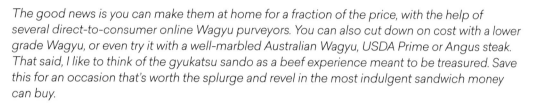

I practically cried the first time I tried a Wagyu katsu sando at Tokyo's Sumibiyakiniku Nakahara (scan the QR code to see it). Just imagine melt-in-your-mouth, gloriously marbled Wagyu beef that's breaded in crunchy panko and flash fried. Sandwich that between fluffy, toasted milk bread slathered with a sweet and tangy tonkatsu sauce for balance and you're in beef heaven. Wagyu katsu sandos (known as gyukatsu sando in Japanese) can run from $80 to $200 at places like Tokyo's famed Wagyumafia, as they use the highest-grade beef. Farms in Japan take immense care in raising the cows and feeding them a rich diet, producing that unparalleled marbling of fat that makes the buttery steaks tender enough to bite right through.

The good news is you can make them at home for a fraction of the price, with the help of several direct-to-consumer online Wagyu purveyors. You can also cut down on cost with a lower grade Wagyu, or even try it with a well-marbled Australian Wagyu, USDA Prime or Angus steak. That said, I like to think of the gyukatsu sando as a beef experience meant to be treasured. Save this for an occasion that's worth the splurge and revel in the most indulgent sandwich money can buy.

Makes 2 Wagyu sandos

1 (8-oz [226-g]) well-marbled Wagyu sirloin, tenderloin or zabuton (bavette) steak, ½–¾ inch (1.3–2 cm) thick

Salt and pepper, to taste

Tonkatsu Sauce

4 tbsp (60 ml) sake

2 tbsp (30 ml) mirin

1 tsp whole black peppercorns

3 tbsp (45 ml) ketchup

2 tbsp (30 ml) Worcestershire sauce, Japanese Bulldog sauce preferred

1 tbsp (15 ml) oyster sauce

½ tsp Japanese hot mustard, Dijon mustard or whole grain mustard

1 tsp honey

Vegetable or canola oil, for frying

4 slices shokupan (Japanese milk bread), substitute with good-quality white bread

Cut the steak into two equal-sized portions and trim off any excess fat on the ends—save this to render beef fat for fried rice or for Jamaican beef patty dough (page 191). If using tenderloin, pound out the steaks to a ¾-inch (2-cm) thickness for more even frying. You can cut the steaks further so they're the same size and shape as the milk bread if you'd like—just save the trimmings to sear and eat on their own or add to fried rice. Season with salt and pepper, then put the steaks back in the fridge—it's best to keep them cold so they stay rare during frying.

In a small saucepan, make the tonkatsu sauce by bringing the sake, mirin and peppercorns to boil over medium heat; cook for 5 to 8 minutes, until it's reduced to a syrupy consistency. Strain out the peppercorns, then whisk in the ketchup, Worcestershire, oyster sauce, mustard and honey. Bring to a boil, then simmer for a couple of minutes until it's a thick, spreadable sauce. Set aside.

Prepare the oil for frying by filling a deep, heavy-bottomed pot with a 1½-inch (4-cm) layer of oil. You can fry the steaks one at a time in a large saucepan to use less oil or use a Dutch oven. Preheat the oil to 340°F (170°C)—frying at a lower temperature slowly raises the internal temperature and prevents a thick grey ring from forming around the edges of the beef.

Meanwhile, toast the milk bread until golden brown then cut off the crusts and set aside.

(continued)

WAGYU KATSU SANDO (CONTINUED)

Katsu Sando

¾ cup (94 g) all-purpose flour

2 eggs, beaten

1¾ cups (190 g) panko bread crumbs

2 tbsp (29 g) Kewpie mayo, optional

Dredge the steaks by first coating them in flour, shaking or brushing off the excess. Then, dip them into a shallow bowl with the beaten eggs and finally, into another bowl with the panko bread crumbs, using your hands to fully coat all sides and edges of the steak.

Fry the breaded cutlet by gently lowering it into the hot oil. Cook until the coating is golden brown, 3½ to 4½ minutes. If the oil is deep enough, you shouldn't need to flip the steak to achieve this. Remove with tongs or a spider and transfer to a paper towel–lined plate to drain the excess oil. Immediately top each cutlet with a fourth of the tonkatsu sauce—adding the sauce when it's fresh out of the fryer prevents it from getting soggy.

Wagyu katsu sando ASSEMBLE! Spread the rest of the tonkatsu sauce evenly on the bottom slices of bread, drizzle on mayo, if desired, then top with the Wagyu cutlet and the top slice of bread. Slice in half and marvel in the swirly white marbling on the perfectly pink Wagyu steak before quickly taking a bite of your crispy, beefy, juicy masterpiece.

#WagyuSando #MeatSweats #IndulgentEatsatHome

Seefood Diet

"I'm on a seafood diet—I see food and I eat it!" This may be an old joke, but it always holds true, and that's especially the case for me and seafood. Growing up in a Filipino household, fish, shrimp, crab and squid were in constant rotation on our dinner table (including the 7UP® Shrimp found on page 133), with countless Filipino seafood dishes thanks to the island geography of the Philippines. And as I traveled to more and more coastal cities and explored NYC's dining scene, my undying love for crustaceans and mollusks became oFISHal, from Southern crawfish boils to Spanish and Portuguese grilled octopus to my fave lobster rolls from NYC seafood institutions Luke's Lobster and Ed's Lobster Bar.

For the cookbook though, I focused on seafood preparations I'm very familiar with but that might not be as mainstream, influenced by my past four years living in Hong Kong. Here my world opened up to the insanely delicious menus of local Cantonese fishing villages, where fresh scallops and shrimp are steamed with garlic and vermicelli, razor clams are stir-fried with black bean sauce and lobsters come with e-fu noodles coated in either scallion and ginger sauce or a high-brow-meets-low-brow processed cheese sauce. But my favorites are the garlicky, spicy Typhoon Shelter-style seafood, which you'll find made with squid on page 140, and the rich Salted Egg Prawns on page 143.

Living in Hong Kong also meant cheap flights to Thailand. There was once a 5-month period where I visited Phuket and Chiang Mai plus Bangkok TWICE thanks to big flight sales. It's these trips that introduced me to Thai grilled seafood with bright cilantro-lime sauce, the best versions of tom yum goong (spicy and sour soup with prawns), and crab yellow curry, as well as the Crispy Noodle-Wrapped Prawns and Giant Crab Omelet that my recipes are based on (page 130 and 134, respectively).

And of course, a seafood chapter wouldn't be complete without mentioning sushi. Japanese food is my favorite cuisine, and each of my five trips to Japan have included mandatory stops at the fish markets in Tokyo, Osaka and Sapporo where the fresh-caught tuna and seafood is often cut and prepared before your very eyes. My Chirashi Bowl on page 137 is my nod to the ones found at these fish markets, and I hope that this chapter helps give you a taste of these experiences while inspiring future travel plans to Asia.

CRISPY NOODLE-WRAPPED PRAWNS
with Pineapple-Chili Sauce

When you love noodles AND seafood, this is the best love child you can ask for! Sure, you can bread and fry shrimp, but these noodle-wrapped prawns bring on the ASMR-worthy CRONCH and satisfying bite that makes fried seafood and crispy fried noodles so dang good. This is a typical Thai preparation, as you can find crispy noodle-wrapped prawns and meatballs at restaurants all over Chiang Mai, Bangkok, Phuket and beyond. While it's usually served simply with sweet chili sauce, I've created two dipping sauce options for your choice of sweet-salty heat or creamy spicy umami to pair with these crispy shrimp for this addictive starter.

Makes 10 to 16 prawns depending on the size of the prawns

Pineapple-Chili Sauce

2 tbsp (30 ml) sweet chili sauce

4 oz (113 g) fresh pineapple, canned crushed pineapple or pineapple chunks in pineapple juice (if in syrup, drain and rinse)

2 tsp (10 ml) fish sauce

1 tsp lime juice

½–1 Thai bird's eye chili, de-stemmed and seeds set aside, minced

Chili Mayo

4 tbsp (58 g) Kewpie mayo

2 tbsp (34 g) tobanjan/doubanjiang (spicy bean paste)

½ tsp rice vinegar

Crispy Noodle-Wrapped Prawns

4–6 oz (113–170 g) thin Chinese egg noodles or shrimp egg noodles

2 lbs (908 g) tiger prawns or jumbo shrimp, deveined and peeled with tails kept on

2 tsp (12 g) salt

2 tsp (12 g) white pepper

Canola oil, for frying

#NoodleWrappedPrawns

#SeefoodDiet

#IndulgentEatsatHome

In a food processor or blender, prepare the pineapple-chili sauce by combining the sweet chili sauce, pineapple, fish sauce, lime juice and chili until smooth, adding some or all of the seeds to reach your desired spice level. Set aside to let the flavors meld while you prepare the shrimp. Alternatively, combine the mayo, tobanjan/doubanjiang and vinegar in a small bowl. I'd recommend trying both sauces to see which you prefer with the crispy fried prawns. Any leftover pineapple-chili sauce goes well with grilled shrimp, chicken, pork, spring rolls and more. You can also use the chili mayo as a dipping sauce or in sandwiches.

Cook the noodles according to package instructions (usually only takes 1 minute!), then drain well and lay them flat on a tray, straightening them out so the noodles don't get too tangled.

Clean the prawns and peel off the shells except the tails, so the prawns are easier to dip. Pat dry then season with the salt and white pepper.

Wrap each prawn with six to eight strands of noodles, starting from the end and working down to the tail. Try to tuck in the ends of the noodles as best you can, but don't worry too much if any noodles stick out as everything will stay together once you fry the prawns.

Preheat a 1½-inch (4-cm) layer of oil in a Dutch oven or other high-walled pan over medium heat while you wrap the prawns. You want it to reach 350 to 375°F (180 to 190°C) so the noodles get super crispy. If you don't have a thermometer, test the oil by throwing in a small piece of a noodle—it should immediately bubble and fry.

Deep-fry the prawns by lowering them into the oil with tongs, a slotted spoon or spider, frying for about a minute until golden brown. Do this in batches so you don't crowd the pan, pausing for a minute or two in between to let the oil come back up in temperature. Transfer to a paper towel–lined tray to absorb excess oil, then transfer to a serving plate and enjoy with your choice of dipping sauce.

SWEET AND GARLICKY 7UP® SHRIMP

7UP? With shrimp? Unless you're Filipino, these are likely the questions you ask yourself reading the title of this recipe, but one taste will make you a believer! 7UP is actually used often in Filipino cuisine since it's very accessible and cheap. You can find it in variations of tocino marinade (page 19), BBQ sauce and here in this garlicky shrimp. It adds a unique, sweet yet acidic flavor and caramelization that is irresistible when mixed with butter and LOTS of garlic. Try it with white rice, stir-fried noodles or even to add an extra flavor explosion to Pineapple Fried Rice (page 148).

Makes 2 to 4 servings

2 lbs (908 g) head-on, shell-on jumbo shrimp, deveined

8 cloves garlic, minced

½ tbsp (3 g) crushed red chili pepper, optional

2 tbsp (30 ml) olive oil

2 tbsp (28 g) unsalted butter

Salt and pepper, to taste

½ cup (120 ml) 7UP or Sprite®

Squeeze of fresh lemon juice, optional

Spiced vinegar (page 22), for dipping, optional

Clean and devein the shrimp, but leave those heads and shells on—that's where all the flavor is! It'll make a huge difference in flavoring the sauce and you'll want to lick off your fingers as you're eating (trust).

In a skillet, cook the garlic and crushed red pepper over low heat with the olive oil and butter, stirring to combine and cooking for 2 to 3 minutes until softened and aromatic. Add the shrimp in a single layer, season with a pinch of salt and fresh ground pepper and cover with the 7UP. Cook over medium-high heat, uncovered, stirring occasionally.

The shrimp are done once the liquid has evaporated, which can take 3 to 7 minutes depending on the width of your pan. Remove from the heat and squeeze a bit of fresh lemon juice on top, if desired. Transfer the shrimp to a platter or serve the shrimp right from the pan as I like to do, that way I can dip the shrimp into the sauce as I peel and eat them 😋. For an extra pop of acidity and spice, try it with a little spiced vinegar.

#7UPShrimp #SeefoodDiet #IndulgentEatsatHome

GIANT CRAB OMELET
with Coconut Curry Sriracha Sauce

If you're reading this, then you've probably watched Netflix's Street Food, a docuseries that explored the chefs behind Asia's street food institutions. I remember being in awe from the first episode, as a badass 74-year-old Thai woman named Jay Fai stood behind two flaming woks, rolling a crab omelet the size of a burrito. We were so enamored that we visited Raan Jay Fai during a trip to Bangkok in 2019, watching her masterful wok skills in person and trying her epic seafood creations.

While the crab and egg shine in Jay Fai's version, I did find myself wanting even more flavor and variations in taste and texture. So instead of simply serving it with sriracha, I've paired it with an easy coconut curry sriracha sauce that's reminiscent of my favorite Thai dish, crab curry. There's a double dose of freshness and acidity from a heavy helping of cilantro and fresh lime juice, plus crunchy fried shallots for a foil to the fluffy omelet. Rolling the omelet takes a little bit of finessing, but it will all be worth it for a taste of Bangkok without the hours-long queue and in the comfort of your own home.

Makes 2 to 4 servings

Coconut Curry Sriracha Sauce

6 tbsp (90 ml) coconut milk

1½ tsp (8 g) Thai yellow or red curry paste

1–3 tbsp (15–45 ml) sriracha, to taste

Juice of 1 lime (save the rest for garnish)

Crab Omelet

1¼ cups (150 g) cooked crab meat

3 cups (720 ml) vegetable oil, for deep-frying

5 eggs, beaten

½ tsp ground white pepper

1 tbsp (15 ml) fish sauce

½ tbsp (4 g) all-purpose flour

Scan the QR code to watch my visit to Raan Jay Fai and see how we outsmarted the hours-long waitlist, then watch how to make my version at home.

First, let's make the coconut curry sriracha sauce to get the easy stuff out of the way. It's as simple as heating the coconut milk with the curry paste in a small saucepan until fully combined, then whisking in the sriracha to your desired heat level. Finish it with a squeeze of lime, then transfer it to a small dipping sauce container on a serving plate while you prepare the crab omelet.

If the crab meat was packed in water, put it in a fine mesh strainer to drain the excess moisture out. I made the mistake of not doing this the first time I made this, and you DO NOT want the oil explosion that resulted 😄.

Preheat the oil in a large saucepan or wok over medium heat while you prepare the rest of the ingredients. You also want to have two spatulas ready to shape the omelet, and a paper towel–lined plate next to the stove for the finished omelet. You may also want to have a wide mesh strainer or colander ready to help drain out the excess oil.

(continued)

Recommended Garnishes

1 bunch fresh cilantro, roughly chopped

2 tbsp (20 g) fried shallots

1 Thai bird's eye chili, chopped

1 lime, quartered

In a large ceramic or heatproof bowl, whisk together the eggs, white pepper, fish sauce and flour. Since there will be a bit of splatter when you pour the omelet into the oil, you don't want to use a plastic bowl for this. Once the eggs are beaten well and are a uniform yellow color, pour 1 to 2 eggs' worth into a ceramic or heatproof measuring cup or mug, which you'll use to fill in any gaps in the omelet as you're shaping it just like Jay Fai does (refer to my video). Then, add the crab meat to the middle of the bowl.

Test the oil temperature—it should read 325°F (160°C) on an instant-read thermometer, or you can stick a wooden chopstick in the oil and see if bubbles form on the outside of the chopstick. Now you're ready to fry!

Carefully add the crab omelet to the oil, making sure to pour the crab into the center part of the omelet. Be careful of any splatters! Let it cook for about 30 seconds, then use the spatulas to roll the omelet against the wall of the pan and push the sides in to form a burrito-like shape. Scan the QR code to watch how it's done.

Keep rolling and pressing the omelet into a tight cylinder, using the spatula to remove any excess pieces that didn't stick to the cylinder. Pour the extra egg from the measuring cup or mug to fill in any parts where the crab is exposed and seal the ends to form a smooth shape. This whole process takes some practice, but watching the videos beforehand will help you visualize the movements.

Fry the omelet until it's golden and crispy, continuing to roll the omelet as it cooks for even color all around. Turn off the heat, then carefully use both spatulas to lift the omelet. To get rid of as much excess oil as possible, first transfer it to a wide mesh strainer or colander to let the oil drip out, then transfer it to the paper towel–lined plate, dabbing excess oil with an additional paper towel, if needed.

Transfer to a serving plate and garnish with fresh cilantro, fried shallots, chili and lime wedges. Squeeze all over with lime and enjoy with the coconut curry sriracha sauce.

#GiantCrabOmelet #SeefoodDiet #IndulgentEatsatHome

CHIRASHI BOWL WITH SALMON ROSES

Sushi is my third favorite food in the world behind pizza and dumplings. There's simply nothing like it, especially when you're able to experience the best-quality fish and seafood through an omakase. You leave the meal up to the sushi master who expertly prepares each nigiri, sashimi, gunkan, temaki or makizushi in front of you in ways that can be intoxicating. Sushi can also be absolutely stunning to look at, from the caviar and ikura-bedazzled omakase boxes at NYC's Kissaki to content creators like Sushi Artisan that create actual masterpieces from sushi.

While most of these types of sushi take great skill to perfect, the humble chirashi bowl is one of the easiest vessels for raw fish and sushi rice that manages to be just as photogenic. You'll find them at fish markets across Japan, in perfectly presented bowls or square "jewelry boxes" filled with cubes of fish and roe sprinkled throughout. There's no need for a bamboo mat or practicing how to correctly press fish and rice into your fingers. All you need is a bowl (ideally a flat, wide one), a sharp knife (which is optional if you get your fish already sliced) and some imagination.

Makes 2 servings

Sushi Rice

1 cup (200 g) uncooked short- or medium-grain rice, look for rice meant for sushi

1–1¼ cups (240–300 ml) water

1 (2-inch [5-cm]) piece kombu, optional

2 tsp (8 g) granulated sugar, optional

2 tbsp (30 ml) rice vinegar, optional

Salt, to taste

Wash the rice. This is a crucial step whenever you make rice, as you want to wash off as much starch as possible so the rice does not become sticky or gummy. Run it under cold water in a bowl while swirling the rice with your hand, pouring out the cloudy water at least six times until the water is mostly clear. You can also put the rice in a fine mesh sieve or colander to wash the rice. Drain as much water as you can, then set aside.

Cook the rice. The best way to do this is in a rice cooker—add enough water until it reaches the 1-cup (240-ml) line marker in the rice cooker pot (typically 1 cup [240 ml] of water). Add a sheet of kombu on top (if using) so it's submerged in the water and rice, then cook according to the rice cooker's settings for white or sushi rice. To make this on a stovetop, bring the rice, 1¼ cups (300 ml) of water and kombu to boil over medium heat in a saucepan that has a tight-fitting lid. Once the water is bubbling all over the top, cover it and turn the heat down to low and cook for another 9 to 11 minutes, until the water has been absorbed. Turn off the heat and leave the pot covered for another 10 to 15 minutes.

Optional: Season the rice. Dissolve the sugar in the rice vinegar. Transfer the hot, cooked rice to a large mixing bowl, then drizzle on the rice vinegar and use a rice paddle or spatula to slice into the rice at 45-degree angles and scoop it so you fold it onto itself to evenly coat the rice in the rice vinegar, then season with salt to taste. Using this slicing method instead of stirring the rice will prevent clumps and help steam escape. To further cool down the rice, you can do this process in front of a fan or use your free hand to manually fan the rice as you slice into it.

(continued)

Cover the rice with a damp towel that is touching the top of the rice so it doesn't dry out. You can choose how cold you want the rice to be by either letting it cool on the countertop or in the fridge to your desired temperature.

Assemble the chirashi bowls. Press the sushi rice into the bottom of the bowl. Now there are a few ways you can lay the fish and seafood for your chirashi bowl depending on if you diced or sliced the fish. You can easily scatter the diced fish across the bowl or lay the slices of fish into your desired pattern. To make roses out of your salmon (or any other fish), you need rectangular slices of at least 2 inches (5 cm) in length. Curl one slice, then continue wrapping more slices around it clockwise to make a rose pattern. Fill the centers of the roses with ikura or another type of fish roe as desired, then decorate the bowl with the remaining garnishes. You can use shiso leaves to hold fish roe or wasabi or slice them into thin ribbons to decorate the bowl. Have fun with the presentation, challenge each other to make the prettiest chirashi bowl, snap a photo and dig into your creation.

#SalmonRoseChirashiBowl #SeefoodDiet
#IndulgentEatsatHome

Chirashi Bowl

4–8 oz (113–226 g) sashimi-grade salmon, sliced if you're making salmon roses, or diced

4–8 oz (113–226 g) your choice sashimi grade fish or seafood, sliced or diced

Optional Garnishes

Ikura, masago or tobiko

Shiso leaves

Sliced cucumber

Takuan (pickled yellow radish)

Furikake

Wasabi and pickled ginger

Edible flowers

Soy sauce

TYPHOON SHELTER SQUID

Get ready for the most addictive calamari ever! With a signature spicy fried bread crumb and garlic topping, Hong Kong's standby seafood is named after the typhoon shelters or small bays where fishermen back in the day would hide out from the stormy weather that hits the island every summer. To this day, you can visit Hong Kong's largest typhoon shelter, Causeway Bay, and enjoy this dish on board small fishing boats (sampan).

You can make almost anything typhoon shelter style, from seafood to chicken wings and even vegetables like enoki mushrooms and eggplant. The most famous version in Hong Kong is with whole crab. It's served at Bourdain-favorites Under Bridge Spicy Crab and Tung Po Kitchen, the latter of which also serves a cheaper typhoon shelter fried fish filet, along with slices of toast so you can scoop the leftover chili garlic bread crumbs straight into your mouth. Shrimp is also common in this dish, which you can make by following the frying technique in my Salted Egg Prawns (page 143) but then cooking with the typhoon shelter toppings below. I absolutely love it with tender-yet-chewy squid to create an extra crunchy, spicy and garlicky version of fried calamari.

Tip: *Double the typhoon shelter toppings for extra crunchy bits to eat with toasted bread, rice or noodles!*

Makes 1 appetizer portion of squid

1 lb (454 g) whole squid (substitute with 12–14 oz [340–397 g] defrosted calamari rings)

Scan the QR code to watch how to clean and cut the whole squid and cook it typhoon shelter style.

Prepare the squid. Warning—this part will feel a bit weird if you have never cleaned a squid before! First, you'll pull the tentacles from the rest of the body; they should all come off in one piece along with the head. Then reach into the hood and pull out all of the entrails, as well as a clear piece inside that feels like plastic (this is called the quill). Cut the fins off the hood, which should also make it easy to peel the purple outer membrane off. Now cut right below the eyes to keep all the tentacles together as one piece, and squeeze near the cut you just made to remove the beak (basically, just remove anything you wouldn't want to eat). From there, depending on the size of the squid, you can cut the tentacles lengthwise to make two or three whole tentacle pieces.

Cut the rest of the squid into rings or bite-sized curls. It's easier to slice them into rings—just slice across the hood to cut it into equal-sized calamari rings. I prefer the bite-sized curls though, as they hold onto the chili garlic bread crumbs better. To create these, stick the knife inside the hood of the squid and slice down from the tip to the opening lengthwise so you're able to open it up flat, laying it so the INSIDE of the hood is facing UP on the cutting board. Now use the knife to create a cross-hatched pattern on the inside of the squid—first, slice diagonal parallel

(continued)

1 tbsp (15 ml) Shaoxing wine

¼ tsp white pepper

Vegetable oil, for frying

2 tbsp (16 g) all-purpose flour

2 tbsp (16 g) cornstarch

2 tbsp (16 g) semolina flour (substitute with cornmeal or 1 tbsp [8 g] each of all-purpose flour and cornstarch)

Small pinch of salt

Typhoon Shelter Toppings

1 tbsp (13 g) fermented black soybeans (*douchi*), rinsed, dried and chopped, optional

4 cloves garlic, minced

2 slices ginger, minced

2 Thai bird's eye chilis, chopped

¾ cup (81 g) panko bread crumbs

⅛ tsp Chinese five spice, optional

Small pinch of salt or MSG, optional

¼ cup (60 g) chopped scallions

lines about half to three-fourths of the way into the flesh across the entire hood going in one direction, making sure not to cut all the way through, and then make equally spaced cuts in the opposite direction to create the pattern. Finally, cut the hood into bite-sized pieces, 1 x 1 inch (2.5 x 2.5 cm) or 2 x 2 inches (5 x 5 cm), depending on how big you want them. They will curl up once you fry them! Rinse everything well in water and let it drain in a colander.

In a small bowl, marinate the squid in the Shaoxing wine and white pepper while you prepare the rest of the ingredients.

In a wok, heat a 1½-inch (4-cm) depth of oil over medium heat until it reaches 325°F (160°C).

Dredge the squid while the oil is heating. In a small bowl, combine the all-purpose flour, cornstarch, semolina flour and salt, then toss the squid into the flour mixture so each piece is evenly coated. You may want to do this in batches to prevent clumps in the dredging.

Fry the squid over medium heat until golden and crispy, about 2 minutes. Do this in batches so you don't crowd the pan, and let the oil come back up to 325°F (160°C) in between batches. Use a spider or slotted spoon to shake off excess oil then set aside the fried squid on a paper towel–lined plate. Carefully scoop out all but ¼ cup (60 ml) of oil from the wok (double or triple this if you're doubling/tripling the recipe), transferring the leftover oil to a heatproof container—you can reuse this by letting it cool, straining out any impurities, then transferring to an airtight container.

Taste a piece of squid before you add any toppings to determine how much more salt you will need in the next step. If it already tastes well seasoned, then you will only need to add a teeny tiny pinch in the next step. You can also use MSG for extra umami.

Make the typhoon shelter toppings by heating the remaining oil in the wok over medium heat. Add the soybeans (if using, for extra salt and umami), garlic, ginger and chilis and cook for 30 seconds to 1 minute until aromatic, then add in the panko bread crumbs and cook until they turn golden brown, tossing frequently to cook evenly.

Add the fried squid, Chinese five spice (if using), salt or MSG to taste and chopped scallions. Toss to coat the squid in the typhoon shelter toppings and transfer it immediately to a serving bowl. Wait a minute before digging into your crunchy, garlicky squid!

#TyphoonShelterStyle #SeefoodDiet #IndulgentEatsatHome

SALTED EGG PRAWNS

If you're familiar with Asian cuisine and especially Asian snacks, then you know that salted egg yolk has been having a moment in recent years. Salted egg yolk potato chips have soared in popularity since expanding beyond their birthplace in Singapore, and you can find salted egg yolk inside or on top of practically every kind of dish in many Asian countries: fried chicken, custard buns, noodles, hot dogs, croissants and, of course, French toast (page 35). While it ALMOST has a truffle oil–like reputation because of its overuse and ease in making things taste good, it's still the MVP in many traditional Cantonese dishes, like these salted egg prawns. Revel in the luxuriously rich, velvety yet just slightly gritty sauce that pairs so addictively with plump, juicy, crispy shrimp.

Makes 8 prawns

Fried Prawns

8 tiger prawns or jumbo shrimp

⅛ tsp salt

¼ tsp white pepper

1 egg white, beaten

3 tbsp (22 g) potato starch or cornstarch

Canola or vegetable oil, for frying

Shrimp Oil (makes 3 tbsp [45 ml] shrimp oil, optional)

3 tbsp (45 ml) canola or vegetable oil

8 shrimp heads and shells

Devein the prawns and peel, if desired, leaving the tail intact and setting aside the shells. Keeping the shells on locks in more flavor, but if you don't want to eat the shells, you can peel them to make it easier to eat—we'll use a trick to keep more of the shrimp flavor in the dish (more on that later).

Season the prawns in salt and white pepper, then refrigerate for 30 minutes. Prepare one small bowl with one beaten egg white (you can use a leftover white from your salted egg yolks!) and another with the potato or cornstarch.

Optional: Make shrimp oil from the prawn heads and shells. Since it's traditional to cook the prawns in their shells to preserve more flavor, making shrimp oil is a great way to keep the flavor and have the ease of eating peeled prawns later. Heat 3 tablespoons (45 ml) of canola or vegetable oil for every 8 prawns over low heat, then add the prawn heads and shells (be careful of splatter!). Continue cooking over low heat while stirring occasionally for 5 to 7 minutes to infuse the oil with shrimp flavor. Prepare a heatproof container with a mesh strainer set on top while the oil is cooking, then pour the oil through the strainer and discard the cooked heads and shells. You'll be left with a vibrant orange oil—let it cool then store in an airtight container in the fridge for up to 4 weeks to use in this recipe, in fried rice, noodles, pasta sauce, shrimp scampi and more.

(continued)

Salted Egg Yolk Sauce

½ tbsp (7 ml) shrimp oil, canola or vegetable oil

1 tbsp (14 g) butter

1 clove garlic, minced

1 stalk curry leaves (substitute with kaffir lime leaves or omit)

1–2 Thai bird's eye chilis, stemmed and seeds set aside

3 Salted Egg Yolks (page 226), steamed and mashed or powdered

2 tbsp (30 ml) evaporated milk

Salt and pepper, to taste

Dredge the prawns by dipping first into the egg white, then into the potato or cornstarch. Shake off any excess and set aside on a small tray or plate. Heat a wok or high-walled skillet with about ½ inch (1.3 cm) of oil over medium heat.

When the oil reaches 300°F (150°C), fry the prawns over medium heat for 1 to 2 minutes per side until they are light golden brown and crispy on the outside, as well as orange and opaque through. Set aside the prawns on a wire rack or paper towel–lined plate and either discard the oil or transfer to a heatproof container to reuse another time.

Make the salted egg yolk sauce by heating the oil and butter over medium heat in the same pan you fried the prawns in. Add the minced garlic, curry leaves and bird's eye chilis, stir-frying until fragrant, about 1 minute. Mix in the Salted Egg Yolks and watch as the mixture starts to froth. Once this happens, add the evaporated milk and cook while mixing constantly until everything comes together into a creamy sauce. Add the salt, pepper and the reserved chili seeds to taste.

Toss the cooked prawns in the sauce until well coated. Transfer to a serving plate and enjoy immediately.

#SaltedEggPrawns #SeefoodDiet #IndulgentEatsatHome

Rice Rice Baby

Is there anything as humble as a bowl of rice? It's the blankest canvas that exists in food and, for many cultures, the cornerstone of every meal. In places like the Philippines and Thailand, it's a means for survival, where meager portions of proteins are purposely cooked to be rich and salty so that the plain white jasmine rice can stretch the dish into enough to feed a family. In South Asia and many parts of the Middle East, long-grain, fluffy basmati rice reigns supreme, paired with rich curries and grilled meats, or with ingredients mixed in to make biryani and jeweled rice, respectively. And while the vast majority of rice dishes start by washing the rice to free it from mush-creating starch, Italy figured out how to use the starch to its advantage by transforming Arborio rice into creamy risotto.

Chances are though, the first dish that comes to mind when you think of rice is fried rice. That's at least the case for me, as I grew up eating garlic fried rice for breakfast and turning leftovers into fried rice whenever I had to fend for myself while my parents were at work. You'll find three versions of fried rice in this chapter with completely different flavor profiles and their own unique, Instagramable presentations, like the pineapple bowl that holds my Thai-style Pineapple Fried Rice (page 148) and the Korean Kimchi Fried Rice Volcano (page 153) that flows out with a lava of egg and cheese. My Crispy Fried Rice Waffles (page 155) includes a recipe for Chinese sausage fried rice (a process that's easy to replicate with any mix-ins so you can also repurpose your leftovers), plus a photogenic technique for transforming any type of leftover rice into crispy rice.

Crispy rice is found around the globe, from Chinese clay pot rice to the *soccarrat* in Spanish paella. Here, I've showcased the bright yellow–hued, now viral version from Iran, Persian Tahdig (page 159), as well as the option to add that coveted bottom-of-the-pot crisp to the fluffy tomato and pepper–infused West African Jollof Rice (page 163) that is so beloved, it's the subject of social media wars.

If crispy rice is on one end of the spectrum, rice porridges like Korean *jook* and Chinese *congee* fall on the other end, where rice gets broken down to make a comforting, soup-like meal. In Filipino cuisine, we have a sweet version called *champorado* that turns glutinous rice into a chocolate rice porridge, but here you'll find my version of Arroz Caldo (page 167), a garlicky chicken soup-meets-congee that will become your savior whenever you feel ill or want a hug in the form of food.

PINEAPPLE FRIED RICE IN A PINEAPPLE

Pineapples are one of the most photogenic foods on the planet. You can find gold cocktail holders and ice buckets shaped like pineapples, pineapple print clothing and, of course, pool floaties. They make you immediately wish you were eating pineapple on a beach, and that's exactly what I'm aiming for with this pineapple fried rice served in a highly 'grammable pineapple bowl. The bold Thai flavors take me right back to the white sand beaches of Phuket, enjoying pineapple fried rice alongside pad Thai and spicy curries.

It's quite easy to make, as most of the work comes from prepping the ingredients that go into it, including cutting the whole pineapple and bright and colorful veggies, though you're welcome to simplify this by using fresh cut or canned pineapple, serving it simply in a bowl and reducing the add-ins for the rice. This recipe also gives you a base technique for making fried rice—substitute the shrimp for another protein (just make sure if you're using chicken or meat to cook it all the way through) and the bell peppers or peas for other veggies. The key when making fried rice is to always try to chop up the veggies to about the same size and add them in based on how long they take to cook (so onions always go in first, peas always go in last).

Makes 2 to 4 servings

Jasmine Rice

3 cups (555 g) cold, day-old jasmine rice, or 1 cup (200 g) uncooked rice if making fresh

Make the jasmine rice at least one day before. No one wants mushy, gummy rice, so fried rice tastes best with cold, day-old rice because the moisture gets dried out in the fridge. The slightly hardened clumps of rice easily break up into individual grains that then get coated in the oil and caramelized on the outside, creating an ideal texture for fried rice. If you're in a time crunch though, I've noted ways you can speed up the process with fresh cooked rice below.

Cook the jasmine rice. Jasmine rice is softer than shorter grain types of rice, so it only needs 1 ⅓ cups (320 ml) of water per 1 cup (200 g) of rice (instead of the more typical 1½ cups [360 ml] of water) to make tender, fluffy rice. Make sure to first wash the rice to remove the starch and minimize any gumminess or stickiness in the cooked rice. Run it under cold water in the pot while swirling the rice with your hand, pouring out the cloudy water at least six times until the water is mostly clear. You can also use a fine mesh sieve or colander to wash the rice. My Zojirushi® rice cooker is my ideal piece of equipment for cooking perfect rice, but if you don't have a rice cooker, you can make this on the stovetop by bringing the rice and water to a simmer over high heat. Once the water is bubbling all over the top, cover it and turn the heat down to low and cook for another 9 to 11 minutes until the water has been absorbed. Turn off the heat and leave it covered for another 10 to 15 minutes, then use a fork to fluff up the cooked rice.

(continued)

Pineapple Fried Rice

1 whole medium pineapple (substitute with 1½ cups [250 g] small pineapple chunks, drained and rinsed in water if using canned pineapple in syrup)

3 tbsp (45 ml) peanut, canola or vegetable oil, divided

6–12 jumbo shrimp, deveined and peeled, substitute with frozen shrimp or omit to make vegetarian (save the shells to make shrimp oil if desired [page 143])

½ onion, chopped

3 cloves garlic, minced

½ red bell pepper, seeded and chopped (substitute with diced carrots if desired)

¼ cup (67 g) cooked ham, optional

½ cup (100 g) green peas, defrosted if frozen

¼ cup (34 g) raw cashews

Let the rice cool by spreading it onto a sheet tray so the steam can escape. It's best to let it cool at room temperature first before transferring to a container to store in the fridge for one or more days to dry out. You can also freeze rice, so you always have it on hand. It lasts in the freezer for 6 to 8 months. Just be sure to thaw it before you stir-fry it. If you're in a time crunch, you can use J. Kenji Lopez-Alt's technique of putting the tray of fresh cooked rice under a fan for at least an hour to dry out the moisture.

Make the pineapple bowl. Slice the pineapple in half with a big sharp knife. Slice on both sides of the pineapple core, then cut the rest of the pineapple into chunks down each side—try not to cut through the skin. Scoop out the pineapple chunks with a large spoon and set aside, discarding the pineapple core. Chop the larger chunks into smaller ones, enough to make 1½ cups (420 g) of pineapple. Store any leftover pineapple in the refrigerator for snacking (I like it with a bit of chili salt or Tajin®), or to make pineapple chili sauce (page 130).

Cook the shrimp (or whatever protein you are using). Heat 1 tablespoon (15 ml) of oil in a wok or large nonstick skillet over medium-high heat. Add the shrimp (if using), cooking for 1 to 2 minutes per side until the shrimp are opaque, then set aside.

Cook the aromatics. Heat another 1½ tablespoons (22 ml) of oil over medium-high heat. Cook the onion until soft and translucent, about 5 minutes, then add the garlic and cook for another minute until fragrant.

Add the bell pepper and cooked ham (if using) and stir-fry for another minute, then add the green peas and cashews and stir-fry for another minute.

Add the rice and, with clean hands, break it up into individual grains as much as possible. Stir-fry for 1 to 2 minutes to toast the rice.

In a small bowl, make the sauce by combining the oyster sauce, fish sauce, bagoong, sriracha, sugar, curry powder and shrimp oil (if using). Add the sauce in a ring around the sides of the wok to evenly distribute it. Stir-fry until the rice is uniformly colored.

Cook the eggs (if using). Make a well in the center of the rice, pushing the rice to the edges of the wok. Heat the rest of the oil in the center of the well, then add the eggs, using a spatula or wooden spoon to break the yolks and scramble the eggs, cooking while stirring just the eggs occasionally to form small, fluffy curds (with the bonus of crisping up the surrounding rice at the same time). Once the eggs are mostly cooked, mix everything together, allowing any uncooked egg to coat the rice.

Add the pineapple and shrimp back in, stir-frying for another minute to heat it.

Add the bird's eye chili and scallions (if using), stir-frying to evenly distribute, then remove from the heat.

Fill the pineapple bowls with fried rice, placing the shrimp on top of the mound of rice. Garnish with chopped cilantro and lime wedges to squeeze onto the rice as desired and enjoy immediately.

#PineappleFriedRice #RiceRiceBaby
#IndulgentEatsatHome

Sauce

1 tbsp (15 ml) oyster sauce or vegetarian oyster sauce

1½ tbsp (22 ml) fish sauce or 1½ tsp (9 g) salt

1 tsp bagoong or shrimp paste (substitute with more oyster or fish sauce or salt)

1 tsp sriracha, sambal or garlic chili sauce, more to taste

1 tsp palm sugar or granulated sugar

½ tsp curry powder, optional

½ tbsp (7 ml) shrimp oil, optional (page 143)

Optional Add-Ins

2 eggs

½ Thai bird's eye chili, chopped

Chopped scallions

Chopped cilantro, for garnish

Lime wedges, for garnish

KIMCHI FRIED RICE VOLCANO

Get ready for an eruption of egg and cheese lava on a volcano of spicy fried rice! Kimchi fried rice or kimchi-bokkeum-bap (김치 볶음밥) is a staple at Korean restaurants and an everyday comfort food since it is cheap and easy to make at home. The main ingredient is kimchi, a spicy fermented cabbage that's essential to Korean cooking and to this satisfying fried rice.

The combination of sour, pungent and spicy kimchi with chewy grains of rice plus traditional Korean seasonings of soy sauce, sesame oil and seaweed is irresistible, especially when paired with Spam®. It may sound off-putting, but it's delicious and incredibly popular in South Korea. During the Korean War, other food items became scarce and U.S. soldiers stationed there would use it as a means of trading around military bases. While you can use bacon or other proteins, I highly recommend even those who are Spam-averse to give it a try in this fried rice. You can also make and serve the fried rice once it's cooked, but for a fun Instagram-worthy plate, turn it into this volcano of fried rice that erupts with flavor.

Makes 2 servings

Kimchi Fried Rice

2 dried shiitake mushrooms

1 (7-oz [196-g]) can Spam, diced, optional (substitute with crispy bacon or Korean bulgogi)

2 tbsp (28 g) butter

½ medium or 1 small onion, diced

2 cloves garlic, minced

1–1½ cups (240–360 g) kimchi, chopped

2 cups (372 g) cold cooked rice (can be same day or day old), ideally short grain (like pearl rice)

2 tbsp (30 ml) kimchi juice, more to taste

1 tsp soy sauce, more to taste

2 tsp (10 ml) sesame oil

1–2 tsp (6–13 g) gochujang for extra spice, optional

Optional Garnishes

Toasted gim or Korean seaweed sheets, shredded (substitute with seaweed snacks, dried shredded nori or furikake)

Sesame seeds

Chopped scallions

If you are using shiitake mushrooms, rehydrate them by placing them in a small bowl and covering it with boiling water. Cover the bowl with a plate to keep the heat from escaping and let it sit for 20 minutes. The shiitake mushrooms will be soft and pliant. Use this time to prep and gather the rest of the ingredients, then feel free to start making the rest of the fried rice while waiting for the mushrooms, as they don't get added in until at least 12 minutes into cooking. Cut off the stems (they're too tough to eat), then chop the mushrooms into small pea-sized pieces.

Cook the Spam (if using) in a medium skillet over medium-high heat for 5 to 7 minutes, tossing occasionally to crisp up on all sides, then set aside.

Melt the butter and cook the onion in the same skillet over medium heat for 5 minutes so it begins to soften, then add the garlic and sauté another minute until aromatic.

Add your desired amount of kimchi, then sauté for 2 to 3 minutes to wilt the kimchi, caramelize the edges and heat it through.

Add the chopped shiitake mushrooms and stir-fry for another minute.

Add the cooked rice, kimchi juice, soy sauce, sesame oil and gochujang (if using) and raise the heat to medium-high. Stir-fry or toss to combine well and heat the rice through. Mix in the crispy Spam and desired garnishes. If you want a layer of crispy rice to mix into the rice, continue cooking for 2 to 3 minutes undisturbed. Remove the pan from the heat.

(continued)

Egg and Cheese "Lava"

4 eggs, beaten

¼–½ cup (57–113 g) shredded low-moisture mozzarella, room temperature, optional

Shape the rice into a volcano by filling a cereal bowl or a deep bowl that will fit all the fried rice, pressing the rice into the bowl to mold the rice. Now take the skillet and put the cooking surface on top of the bowl, positioning the bowl in the center of the skillet. Flip the whole thing over and gently shimmy the bowl off to reveal a mound of rice in the center of the skillet. Put the skillet back on low heat, then use a spoon to gently press a crater into the center of the mound, as well as a path on the side of the "volcano" for the egg "lava" to flow down through.

Pour the beaten eggs into the crater and watch the "lava" flow out into the outer ring of the skillet. If desired, add the mozzarella cheese to the center of the crater and down the side of the volcano.

Cover with a lid for 3 to 4 minutes until the eggs are cooked and the cheese is melted. Serve as is, digging into the volcano to get some cheese and egg with each bite, or mix everything together, adding more garnishes as desired. Just make sure to use a wooden or plastic spoon if you used a nonstick skillet so you don't scratch the pan!

#KimchiFriedRiceVolcano #RiceRiceBaby
#IndulgentEatsatHome

CRISPY FRIED RICE WAFFLES

If you love crispy rice, then say hello to THE best way to reheat leftover fried rice! While many of the recipes in this section have you cook the rice over direct flame to create the crispy scorched bottom of the pot, aka tahdig (page 159), we're repurposing the waffle maker to easily make crispy rice with a fun presentation. It works even better when the rice is cold, so it makes reheating leftovers just as easy as using the microwave, but with the benefit of getting crispy rice.

Don't have leftover fried rice? Try making this Chinese sausage fried rice, which uses lap cheong to add sweet, smoky, savory flavor to fried rice. You can also use this recipe as a base to make other kinds of fried rice. Just remember to always cook the aromatics first (like garlic and onion), then stir-fry any proteins and/or vegetables, add the cold day-old rice (which makes the best fried rice thanks to its lower moisture content), include the seasonings and, finally, make the well in the middle to cook the eggs right in the pan and save yourself from washing another bowl.

Makes 2 servings

Chinese Sausage Fried Rice (substitute with any leftover rice you have)

2 tbsp (30 ml) vegetable, canola or peanut oil

2 cloves garlic, minced

3 oz (85 g) lap cheong, cut lengthwise then chopped

1 cup (135 g) frozen green peas, thawed in water then drained well

3 cups (558 g) cold day-old rice

½ tbsp (7 ml) oyster sauce

½ tbsp (7 ml) light soy sauce

½ tbsp (7 ml) dark soy sauce (substitute with light soy sauce)

1 tsp sesame oil

¼ tsp white pepper

2 large eggs

Salt and pepper, to taste

If you are using leftover rice, skip ahead to the "To make the waffles" step on the next page.

Optional: Make the Chinese sausage fried rice. Heat a wok over medium-high heat, then add the oil. Once the oil is shimmering, add the garlic and cook for 30 seconds until fragrant. Add the lap cheong and peas, and stir-fry until heated through, about 2 minutes.

Break up the rice into individual grains with clean hands before adding it to the wok, then add the sauces and sesame oil in a ring around the sides of the wok to evenly distribute it and sprinkle on the white pepper. Stir-fry until the rice is uniformly colored.

Make a well in the center of the rice, pushing the rice to the edges of the wok. Add the eggs into the well, using a spatula or wooden spoon to break the yolks and scramble the eggs, cooking while stirring just the egg occasionally to form small, fluffy curds (with the bonus of crisping up the surrounding rice at the same time). Once the eggs are mostly cooked, mix everything together, allowing any uncooked egg to coat the rice.

Add salt and pepper to taste, then serve as is or transfer to a tray to cool if you want to make the waffles. If you want the rice to be extra crispy, it should be cold before it goes into the waffle maker—let the fried rice cool at room temperature before storing in the refrigerator for up to 3 days.

(continued)

CRISPY FRIED RICE WAFFLES (CONTINUED)

Fried Rice Waffles

Cooking spray or oil spray

2–4 cups (260–600 g) leftover fried rice

Fried egg and garnished as desired

To make the waffles, preheat the waffle maker until the light indicator shows that it's hot. Spray the cooking surface with cooking spray or oil so the fried rice waffles will easily slip out when cooked.

Pack the fried rice into a bowl or other round container—this will make it easier to add to the waffle maker.

Flip the fried rice container onto the center of the waffle maker, jiggling the container to reveal a mound of rice, then use a spoon to shape it to fill the waffle maker. Close the top down—for deep grooves and a crispier texture, use force to press down on the waffle maker as much as possible to compact the rice. If you want to keep a middle layer of fluffier rice, press down just enough to flatten the rice and leave an imprint of the waffle maker.

Cook for at least 4 minutes. You can lift the top to check on how the rice is crisping up. Once you've achieved your desired crispiness, open the waffle maker and put a plate directly onto the waffle, then carefully flip to transfer the waffle onto the plate. If your waffle maker doesn't allow you to flip one side over, then use tongs to lift the fried rice waffle out and slide a plate underneath it.

Serve immediately, using a fork to listen to the crispy exterior and topping with a fried egg and garnishing as desired.

#CrispyFriedRiceWaffle #RiceRiceBaby #IndulgentEatsatHome

TAHDIG (PERSIAN CRISPY RICE)

with Saffron Yogurt Lamb Chops

In my mind, tahdig must have been named after the phrase "TAH-DAH!" since you're bound to say it to your guests when you flip over the pan to reveal the dome of crispy rice! In actuality, the Persian word tahdig *(pronounced tah-DEEG) means "bottom of the pot," in reference to that crispy layer of rice that develops at that location. I first tried it at Zahav, star Israeli chef Michael Solomonov's flagship restaurant in Philadelphia. I remember being stunned by the dome of Persian rice that landed on the table, paired with a mouthwatering slow-roasted pomegranate lamb shoulder that became a must whenever we visited Philly. My version of tahdig is a nod to Zahav's, as I pair a traditional preparation of crispy rice coated with saffron butter with easier-to-find lamb chops that have been marinated in a bright saffron, garlic and onion–infused yogurt, all topped with bright pops of pomegranate seeds and crunchy pistachios.*

Makes 3 to 4 servings

Saffron Tea

1 tsp saffron threads

Pinch of coarse salt, optional

1 cup (240 ml) hot water

Saffron Yogurt Lamb Chops

¾ cup (170 g) plain yogurt

½ medium onion

4 cloves garlic, peeled

1 tbsp (15 ml) lemon juice

1 tsp salt

1 tsp fresh ground pepper

1 tbsp (15 ml) olive oil, plus more for greasing the pan

8 lamb chops

Make the saffron tea—we will use this for both the lamb chop marinade and the tahdig. You can also use this technique (minus the salt) to make saffron tea for drinking, as it has great health benefits (just Google it!). If you have a mortar and pestle, then use it to grind the saffron and coarse salt into a powder to release as much flavor as possible, though you can skip this step if you don't have one. Put the saffron threads or powdered saffron in a small glass container and pour the hot water over. Let it sit for 15 to 20 minutes until it turns a vibrant orange. If you are not making the tahdig until the next day, reserve 2 tablespoons (30 ml) of saffron tea to marinate your lamb chops in the next step, then store the remaining saffron tea in a container in the fridge to use for your tahdig. Otherwise, set aside.

Marinate the lamb chops. Add all the marinade ingredients for the lamb chops including 2 tablespoons (30 ml) of saffron tea into a food processor or blender and blend until smooth. Add the lamb chops to a resealable silicon bag or zip-top bag along with the marinade, tossing around to coat evenly. Marinate in the refrigerator for 4 to 12 hours, the longer the better to let the flavors penetrate the lamb. Remove it from the fridge an hour and a half before you plan to eat and 30 minutes before starting on the tahdig. Strain the lamb chops from the marinade, using your hand or a spoon to wipe off excess marinade from the surface and bones. Discard the marinade and leave the lamb chops on the counter to come to room temperature while you prepare the tahdig.

(continued)

Tahdig (Persian Crispy Rice)

2 cups (370 g) basmati rice

1–2 tbsp (17–34 g) salt

2 tbsp (28 g) plain yogurt

4 tbsp (60 ml) grapeseed, canola or vegetable oil, divided

4 tbsp (56 g) butter, sliced

To make the tahdig, we first need to par-cook the rice. Add the rice to a large pot. Put the pot under running water in the sink and wash the rice by using your hand to swirl the rice in the water, carefully dumping out the cloudy water each time. Do this five or six times until the water is mostly clear. Now fill the pot with water so that the rice has at least 4 inches (10 cm) of water above it. Bring it to a boil over high heat, and once the water is boiling, add 1 to 2 tablespoons (17 to 34 g) of salt (depending on how seasoned you want your rice to be) and reduce the heat to medium-high. Let this cook for 5 to 6 minutes to par-cook the rice until it's al dente. Test this by tasting a grain of rice—it should be soft on the outside with a slight bite on the inside. You can also squeeze it between your fingers; the outside should smush, but the inside should still be intact. Once it gets to this texture, remove it from the heat and use a fine-mesh strainer or colander to drain any excess water, running the rice under cold water to stop it from cooking.

If you are grilling the lamb chops, preheat the grill now so it has time to get hot while you prepare the tahdig.

Assemble the tahdig. Take 1½ cups (255 g) of the par-cooked rice and combine it well with the yogurt, 2 tablespoons (30 ml) of saffron tea and 2 tablespoons (30 ml) of oil. Get a 10-inch (25-cm) lidded nonstick pot or skillet and generously coat the bottom and sides with the rest of the oil, then spread the yogurt-rice mixture evenly on the bottom of the pan all the ways to the edges. Add the rest of the par-cooked rice on top, forming a slight mound in the center of the pan. Now we want to poke holes in the rice which will help steam escape as it cooks. Take the end of a wooden spoon or a wide chopstick and poke a hole in the center of the mound, almost to the bottom of the rice, and then poke two rings of holes around the center hole, as pictured. Distribute the butter evenly across the top, between the holes, then drizzle the rest of the saffron tea all over.

Cook the tahdig by heating the entire pan over low heat. Wrap the lid with a clean kitchen towel to absorb any steam, using a rubber band to tie the ends around the handle so that the kitchen towel doesn't accidentally catch on fire. Cook it for 35 to 45 minutes, rotating every so often to make sure it browns evenly. You can use a spatula to push in on the edges and peer in to see if the bottom of the rice is browned to your desired level of crispiness.

(continued)

Garnish

½–1 cup (70–140 g) pomegranate seeds

¼ cup (6 g) loosely packed fresh parsley, chopped

¼ cup (28 g) shelled pistachios, chopped

Cook the lamb chops during the last 10 to 15 minutes of tahdig cooking time. You want to cook them until browned on the outside and an instant-read thermometer inserted into the thickest part of the meat registers 145°F (60°C) for a perfectly pink inside (feel free to cook for longer to achieve desired doneness). If you need to work in batches or if the lamb chops are done before the tahdig, you can keep the cooked lamb chops in a 200°F (90°C) oven to keep them warm while you work. Otherwise, set aside the cooked lamb chops on a plate or tray and cover with foil to rest.

Option 1: Grill the lamb chops. Cook on the grill for 4 to 5 minutes per side without disturbing so they develop dark grill marks, making sure to keep them away from the hottest part of the grill to they don't burn.

Option 2: Pan sear the lamb chops. Heat a cast-iron skillet or grill pan to medium-high heat, then brush all over with olive oil. Add the lamb chops, pressing them into the pan to develop a nice sear, and cook for 3 minutes without disturbing. Flip and sear another 2 to 3 minutes until cooked.

Option 3: Air fry the lamb chops. Preheat the air fryer to 390°F (200°C). Brush or spray the bottom of the basket with olive oil, then arrange the lamb chops in a single layer without overlapping. Air fry for 4 minutes, then flip and cook another 4 minutes, or until cooked.

The BIG REVEAL. Remove the lid from the tahdig and use a spatula to loosen the edges of the rice. Get a plate that's larger than the opening of your pan and flip it upside down onto the pan so it can catch the tahdig when you flip everything over. You should probably grab some oven mitts or kitchen towels in case the handle(s) of your pan are too hot. Now keep a firm hold of the plate onto the opening of the pan, and flip the entire thing over on one big, confident movement like you own that tahdig! Give it a few shimmies or taps to help the tahdig release, then remove the pan to reveal your (hopefully) fully intact layer of crispy, golden rice. If anything DID manage to stick, just use a spatula to scrape it out and place it back onto the tahdig like nothing ever happened.

Serve the tahdig with the lamb chops, topping it all with pomegranate seeds, chopped parsley and pistachios before breaking into that golden layer and serving each person a mound of crispy and fluffy rice along with two or three lamb chops.

#Tahdig #RiceRiceBaby #IndulgentEatsatHome

WEST AFRICAN JOLLOF RICE

Jollof rice is simultaneously the unifier and divider of West Africa. It's known as "Party Rice" since a big pot of this spiced tomato, pepper and onion–infused rice can be found at every gathering across the nations of Ghana, Senegal, Cameroon, Nigeria, Sierra Leone, Togo, Mali, Benin, The Gambia and Côte d'Ivoire, resulting in a deep love for the dish. But with that, comes INTENSE pride over whose version is best. It was invented by the Wolof people of Senegal and The Gambia, but the root of most #JollofWars social media debates is between Ghana and Nigeria. While I won't be the judge on whose version is best, I can tell you that THIS jollof, based on countless Nigerian jollof rice recipes I researched along with tips from my followers, is DAMN GOOD. Trust me when I say you're going to want to make a big pot of it, as it'll be tough to stop eating this vibrantly flavored rice and juicy chicken.

Makes 3 to 6 servings

Obe Ata (Nigerian Red Sauce)

14 oz (397 g) canned whole peeled tomatoes with juices

1 large red bell pepper, stemmed, seeded and roughly chopped

1–2 Scotch bonnet, habanero or other spicy chilis, stemmed and roughly chopped

3 cloves garlic

1 (1-inch [2.5-cm]) piece ginger, peeled and roughly chopped

½ red onion, roughly chopped

½ tsp chicken bouillon (½ a standard cube)

2 tbsp (30 ml) canola or vegetable oil

Pan-Seared Chicken (optional)

1 chicken bouillon cube, crumbled, or 1 tsp chicken powder

2 tsp (6 g) paprika

2 tsp (6 g) dried thyme

1½ tsp (4 g) garlic powder

1½ tsp (4 g) ground ginger

1 tsp turmeric

1 tsp salt

1 tsp ground pepper

6 pieces skin-on chicken thighs and/or drumsticks (bone-in or boneless both work)

Make the obe ata up to 3 days before you plan to serve the jollof rice. Use a blender or food processor to pulse and then blend all the ingredients except the canola oil until smooth, working in batches, if needed.

Tip: To make the rice without the chicken, add a pinch of all the chicken spices to your obe ata during this step.

Transfer the obe ata to a large saucepan or skillet (I like to use my Le Creuset braiser for maximum surface area) and bring to a boil over medium heat. Simmer for 30 to 40 minutes until most of the liquid has evaporated and the mixture has turned brick red in color. Then add the oil to the pan to fry the obe ate over medium heat for 1 to 2 minutes, which intensifies the flavor even more. If you are making ahead, let it cool at room temperature completely before covering and storing in the refrigerator in an airtight container for 3 to 4 days. If you are making the obe ata the same day as the jollof rice, then make sure to follow the next steps for marinating the chicken a day or two before making the obe ata.

Marinate the chicken by first combining all the spices in a small bowl, using your fingers to crumble the bouillon cube with the spices, as the friction will help break up the bouillon cube. Rub the mix all over the chicken, getting into all the crevices. Marinate covered in the refrigerator the night before making the jollof rice, or even better, for 24 to 48 hours before so the flavors can fully penetrate.

(continued)

WEST AFRICAN JOLLOF RICE (CONTINUED)

Start the jollof rice by cooking the chicken with the skin side down over medium heat in a large Dutch oven or large oven-safe pan with a tight-fitting lid, positioning the pieces so they're right next to each other. You don't need to add any oil to the pan as the chicken skin will render out a lot of fat. Don't touch the chicken pieces for 8 to 10 minutes to let them develop a nice sear on the skin—it will release from the pan on its own as the fat renders.

Wash the rice while the chicken is cooking. Run it under cold water in a bowl while swirling the rice with your hand, pouring out the cloudy water at least six times until the water is mostly clear. You can also use a fine mesh sieve or colander to wash the rice. Drain as much water as you can then set aside.

Flip over the chicken once you have nice browning on the chicken skin and sear the other side for 2 minutes. Then transfer the half-cooked chicken back to the container it was marinating in for now—it will finish cooking in the oven with the jollof rice. Speaking of which, this is a good time to preheat the oven to 350°F (180°C) so it's ready for later.

Cook the red onion and bay leaf in the Dutch oven. First, melt the butter in the chicken fat (or with the olive oil if omitting the chicken) over medium-low heat, then add the red onion and bay leaf. Cook for 6 to 8 minutes until the onion is soft—this part will smell absolutely amazing!

Mix in the tomato paste and curry powder (if using) and raise the heat to medium, cooking while stirring for 5 to 7 minutes until the tomato paste has turned brick red. Add the obe ata and stir to fully combine, cooking for another 2 to 3 minutes.

(continued)

Jollof Rice

2¾ cups (500 g) washed parboiled long-grain rice (like Uncle Ben's™ or Carolina Gold®), basmati rice or jasmine rice

2 tbsp (28 g) unsalted butter

1 tbsp (15 ml) olive oil, optional (use if omitting the chicken)

1 red onion, chopped

1 dried bay leaf

2 tbsp (34 g) tomato paste

½ tsp African or Caribbean curry powder, optional

1½ cups (360 ml) chicken stock, plus more if needed

Add the chicken stock to the Dutch oven and give it a stir. Bring to a boil, then simmer covered for 10 minutes so the chicken stock infuses into the stew.

Add the rice, and, if needed, add more chicken stock. You want the liquid to just cover the top of the rice after stirring everything together.

Gently place the chicken on top of the rice in an even layer with the skin side up. Don't worry if it sinks into the rice a little, it will all cook just fine.

Cover the Dutch oven with two layers of aluminum foil or parchment paper, then fit on the lid. You want a tight seal so that the rice steams in the pot to get fluffy. Bake for 35 minutes, then remove from the oven and keep the lid on for another 15 minutes (no peeking!) to help the rice continue to fluff.

Fluff the rice by removing the lid and using tongs to set aside the chicken so you can use a fork to fluff up the rice in the pot. Since the chicken pushes down on the liquid, there may be some excess stew on the top layer of rice, so just mix that into the rest of the rice to evenly distribute.

Want to get scorched rice on the bottom of the pot? Put the pot back on the stovetop covered for 5 minutes over medium heat. You'll hear the rice sizzle as it toasts and crisps on the bottom layer, and this will finish fluffing up the rest of the rice.

Want to crisp up the chicken skin? Transfer the chicken to a baking tray and broil for 1 to 2 minutes in the oven on high or give it 2 minutes in the air fryer at the highest temperature it can go.

Serve the jollof rice by placing the chicken back on top of the rice and let everyone dig in to get a big scoop of rice and chicken.

#JollofRice #RiceRiceBaby #IndulgentEatsatHome

ARROZ CALDO
(Filipino Rice Porridge)

Feeling under the weather? A little hungover? Let me introduce you to the most comforting cure, arroz caldo. This Filipino rice porridge is what my mom would make to heal all ailments, from colds to tummy problems. Unlike its Chinese counterpart, congee, which is usually white in color and primarily flavored by its toppings, arroz caldo or "rice broth" in Spanish has a garlicky, ginger-spiked, beige base of rice cooked in rich chicken stock. It's sometimes colored bright yellow from the addition of kasubha or safflower, a cheaper alternative to saffron.

On top of that, arroz caldo gets even more flavor from the garnishes—typically fried garlic, scallions, a drizzle of fish sauce, squeeze of calamansi (a Filipino citrus) or lemon—and hard-boiled eggs. We're going to soft boil the eggs instead for a perfectly jammy yolk and add crispy chicken skin (though you can omit or substitute with store-bought fried pork rinds for convenience). The key to making the best arroz caldo is using both jasmine rice, which breaks apart in the stock to thicken the soup, and glutinous rice, which retains its shape more to create a combination of textures.

Makes 6 small bowls or 3 large bowls

1 whole medium-sized chicken, cut into pieces (substitute with 3 lbs [1.3 kg] skin-on chicken wings and thighs)

6 cups (1.4 L) water

1 tbsp (15 ml) canola or vegetable oil

9 cloves garlic, minced, divided

1 large onion, chopped

1 (1½-inch [4-cm]) piece ginger, peeled and julienned

½ cup (100 g) uncooked jasmine rice

½ cup (100 g) uncooked glutinous rice (substitute with jasmine rice for a soupier porridge)

3 tbsp (45 ml) fish sauce, more to taste

Salt and white pepper, to taste

Remove the chicken skin from the chicken breasts of the whole chicken, or from two chicken thighs. Chop it into tiny pieces—you will use this to make the crispy chicken skin topping later.

Cook the chicken and make stock. Place the chicken in a large pot and submerge it in the water. Bring to a boil over medium heat, then reduce to a simmer over medium-low, skimming any scum from the surface. Cook for 40 to 50 minutes until the chicken is fully cooked. You can check this by cutting into the chicken—the juices should run clear. Remove the chicken and set aside.

Cook the crispy chicken skin. Heat the oil in a pot over medium-low heat, then add the chicken skin and cook while stirring until it's golden brown and crispy, 5 to 7 minutes. Transfer to a paper towel–lined plate, leaving the oil and rendered fat in the pot.

Make the fried garlic. Add a third of the garlic to the hot oil and cook while stirring. Remove it once it's starting to turn golden brown—it will continue cooking after it's removed from the oil, and you don't want it to burn and turn bitter in flavor. Transfer to the paper towel–lined plate next to the crispy chicken skin.

(continued)

ARROZ CALDO (CONTINUED)

Garnishes

3–6 large eggs

Calamansi halves (substitute with lemon wedges)

Fried garlic

Chopped scallions

Crushed chicharron (fried pork rinds), optional

Cook the aromatics. Add the onion to the remaining hot oil and cook until soft and translucent, 5 to 7 minutes. Add the remaining garlic and ginger and cook until fragrant, another minute or two.

Add the rice and stir to coat, toasting for a minute or two before adding the chicken stock and fish sauce. Bring to a boil, then reduce the heat to low and cover, simmering for 20 to 30 minutes while stirring occasionally (try to scrape from the bottom to keep the rice from burning) until the rice has reached your desired consistency.

Shred the chicken while the arroz caldo is simmering, discarding the skin and bones. Set aside.

Soft boil the eggs. Boil a small saucepan of water over medium-high heat, then adjust the heat to low and use a slotted spoon to gently add the eggs to the water. Set a timer for 6 minutes for a slightly runny, jammy egg yolk and a fully set egg white, adding more time depending on how cooked you want the yolk to be. Prepare a bowl of ice water while the eggs are cooking so that once the timer goes off, you can use a slotted spoon to transfer the eggs to the ice bath to stop them from cooking and make them easier to peel. Slice them in half to add to the arroz caldo when it's done.

Add the chicken to the arroz caldo—I like to reserve a small handful to add some pieces to the top of the bowl so it's visible for presentation. Stir to reheat the chicken, then taste the porridge and season with more fish sauce, salt and white pepper, as desired.

Ladle the arroz caldo into bowls and top with your chosen garnishes, leaving small bowls of garnish on the side to add more as desired. To store leftovers, let the ungarnished arroz caldo come to room temperature first, then transfer to an airtight container and store in the fridge for 3 to 5 days, adding water or chicken broth as needed to thin out the porridge when you reheat it.

#ArrozCaldo #RiceRiceBaby #IndulgentEatsatHome

Pockets of Love

We've saved the best of the savory dishes for last, as this is actually my favorite section of the book. There's something so comforting about dumplings, meat pies and other #PocketsofLove, both in creating and eating them. The act of using your hands to knead, roll and pleat the dough is therapeutic, which is so needed when the world seems to be going awry. It's also a wonderful communal activity—the bonds you make while chatting with flour-covered hands and subsequently sitting down to enjoy your masterpieces are unmatched.

So, it should come as no surprise that almost every culture has their version of a dumpling. Chinese *siumai* and *xiao long bao*, Japanese *gyoza* (page 172), Italian ravioli, Jamaican Beef Patties (page 191), Korean *mandu*, Puerto Rican *pastelitos* (known in other Latin American countries as empanadas [page 177]), Russian *pelmeni*, Jewish matzo balls, Nepali Momo (page 187) and more. They can be boiled, panfried, steamed, deep-fried or cooked in broth for a playground of textures and filled with anything your heart desires, from traditional meat fillings to fusion fillings like buffalo chicken or lamb masala (page 185).

But my real favorite part about making dumplings? The leftovers. All the recipes in this section are made for freezing so you can feel the love up to 3 months after you put in the hard work. Go ahead and make a big batch knowing you'll have the perfect snack, breakfast, lunch or dinner in less time than it would take you to decide what to order from a delivery app.

GYOZA SKILLET with Crispy Wings

Dumplings are amazing as is, but there's something EXTRA special about an entire plate covered in crispy bottoms with every gap filled with golden brown "wings" that gives a satisfying crunch when you pull each gyoza off the plate. Gyoza are the traditional Japanese version of dumplings, typically with thinner skins than the Chinese versions, filled with ground pork and heavier accents of cabbage and ginger, and almost exclusively panfried instead of boiled or steamed. This particular style is called hanetsuki gyoza (hane translates to wings). Panfried dumplings are my favorite kind of dumplings, thanks to that combination of textures that's a party in your mouth when combined with that juicy pork filling. They especially sing when paired with a vibrant ponzu-based dipping sauce accented by one of my favorite ingredients ever, yuzu kosho—a Japanese citrus and pepper paste that brightens anything it's added to with notes of grapefruit and lime plus heat from the chili. After you master these gyoza, have fun experimenting with different dumpling fillings since you can use the pleating and crispy lattice techniques on your chosen dumplings.

Makes 30 to 40 gyoza for 2 to 3 plates with crispy lattice

Gyoza Filling

8 oz (226 g) ground pork

3 oz (85 g) cabbage, stems and core removed and very finely chopped

2–3 (about 1 oz [28 g]) dried shiitake mushrooms rehydrated in hot water, stems removed and finely chopped

1 (0.5-oz [14-g]) bulb garlic chives or scallions, green tops only, finely chopped

1 clove garlic, finely minced

1 (½-inch [1.3-cm]) piece ginger, finely minced

1 tbsp (15 ml) soy sauce

1 tbsp (15 ml) sake

1 tbsp (15 ml) sesame oil

½ tbsp (5 g) white pepper

¼ tsp salt

Make the gyoza filling. In a large bowl, combine the pork, cabbage, mushrooms, chives, garlic, ginger, soy sauce, sake, sesame oil, pepper and salt. For easier prep, you can add roughly chopped cabbage, scallions, ginger and garlic to a food processor and pulse until finely chopped, then mix with the ground pork. Cook a spoonful of the meat in a skillet to taste for flavor and adjust the salt and other spices as desired.

Prepare your gyoza folding area by placing the pile of dumpling wrappers on your work surface and underneath a damp kitchen towel to prevent them from drying out. I like to put them on a big tray so I can also keep the folded dumplings under the damp towel. Place a small bowl of water nearby.

(continued)

Panfried Gyoza

30–40 gyoza wrappers, thawed, if frozen

1 tbsp (15 ml) canola or neutral oil

Crispy Lattice Slurry

½ cup (120 ml) water

1 tsp unseasoned rice vinegar

1 tsp cornstarch

1–2 tsp (8–16 g) all-purpose flour, for a crunchier lattice, or rice flour for a more delicate lattice

2 tsp (10 ml) sesame oil

To begin assembling the dumplings, place a gyoza wrapper in the middle of your nondominant hand, then use chopsticks or a measuring spoon to add a heaping teaspoon of filling to the center of the dumpling. I like to shape the filling into a football so it's easier to fold the wrapper around it. Now dip one of your fingers on your dominant hand into the water and wet the edges of the wrapper around the filling—this will turn the flour coating your wrappers into "glue"!

To fold the gyoza, start by folding in half like a taco so that the pointed edges of the "football" of filling are on the ends of your taco. Pinch together the center of your taco where the edges meet. Then use your thumbs or index fingers to pull the one side of the right end of the wrapper toward the center to form a small pleat, repeating down the edge of the wrapper so you have three pleats on the right side. Now repeat on the left side, pulling the wrapper toward the center in the opposite direction, forming three pleats on that side. Press the edges, using a dab of water if necessary to seal the edges. Place the completed dumpling under the damp kitchen towel or paper towels and continue folding dumplings until you use all the filling.

Make the crispy lattice slurry by whisking together the water, vinegar, cornstarch and flour in a measuring cup so it's easy to pour into the pan later.

To panfry the gyoza, add the canola oil to a 9- to 10-inch (23- or 25-cm) nonstick or cast-iron skillet that has a lid, ideally a glass one so you can peek inside as it's cooking. Heat over medium-high, then once the oil is shimmering, add the gyoza to the pan by pressing each one into the oil, then moving it to form a circular pattern as pictured, starting from the outside ring and filling into the center. Panfry them for 1 to 2 minutes until the bottoms begin to turn golden brown.

Add the slurry to the pan, giving it one last whisk just before adding and pouring it to fill in the gaps between the dumplings (be careful of splatters!). Cover with the lid so that the water in the slurry steams to cook the tops of the dumplings. Cook over medium-low heat for 5 minutes or until the gyoza skins look translucent.

Make the dipping sauce while the dumplings cook. In a bowl, add the vinegar, sesame oil, yuzu (if using), soy sauce, chili oil and scallions (if using). Yuzu kosho is quite salty and packs some heat, so I'd recommend starting with 1 tablespoon (15 ml) of soy sauce and tasting before adding additional soy sauce or chili oil. Feel free to adjust the seasonings to taste and write down your personal ratios for next time.

Now let's crisp up the lattice. Remove the lid from the pan and continue cooking until the white slurry starts to crisp up. When this happens, use a spoon to drizzle the sesame oil around the edges of the pan, which will help loosen the crispy lattice and add flavor. Once the water is fully evaporated and the lattice has reached your desired crispiness and golden-brown color, gently shake the pan to loosen the dumplings, using chopsticks or a spatula to loosen the edges, if needed. Remove from the heat.

To plate the gyoza, you have two options. To show off the crispy bottoms, get a plate that's just smaller than your skillet but big enough to fit all the dumplings. Firmly press the plate against the dumplings with one hand, holding the skillet handle with your other, then carefully flip the entire skillet over to reveal the plate full of dumplings—be careful as there could be remnants of oil that can spill off the pan when you flip. If you're uncomfortable with this, you can slide the dumplings off the skillet onto a plate instead and then place a bigger plate on top to do the flipping action if you still want to show the crispy bottoms.

Serve the gyoza with the dipping sauce on the side and enjoy!

#GyozaSkillet #PocketsofLove #IndulgentEatsatHome

Dipping Sauce

2 tbsp (30 ml) unseasoned rice vinegar

1 tsp sesame oil

⅛ tsp yuzu kosho, optional (adjust the soy sauce to taste, if using)

1–2 tbsp (15–30 ml) soy sauce

1–2 tsp (5–10 ml) Japanese chili oil (la-yu), optional (substitute with Sichuan Chili Crisp Oil [page 229])

1 tbsp (15 g) chopped scallions, optional

CHEESY PORK AND PLANTAIN EMPANADAS
with Spicy Green Sauce

Empanadas are my absolute favorite non-Asian dumpling. In Buenos Aires, they're typically filled with a spiced filling of ground beef, green olives and hard-boiled eggs and are more often baked than fried. In Puerto Rico, they're called pastelillos or empanadillas, and the spiced ground beef is often cooked with a bold pepper-based sofrito and potatoes. But my obsession with them is truly thanks to NYC institution Empanada Mama, a 24-hour Colombian diner that I used to live down the street from that served golden fried half-moons paired with their signature green sauce, a spicy jalapeño-based sauce similar to Peruvian aji verde and Cuban mojo verde.

This green sauce is also what makes all the difference in one of my favorite sandwiches in NYC, the Pernil with a Twist from Sophie's Cuban that inspired this empanada. Juicy roast pork, sweet plantains (maduros), sautéed onions and green sauce create a savory, garlicky and slightly sweet combination that's perfect sandwiched between toasted bread. Here, we're stuffing it into a crispy, flaky empanada along with mozzarella cheese for extra cheese-pulls and a rich contrast to the vibrant green sauce that is known to win over even the staunchest cilantro and mayo haters.

Tip: *Try filling your empanada discs with leftover ingredients from my other recipes in the book—think empanadas stuffed with breakfast mac and cheese, longganisa and scrambled egg, Korean fried chicken and mozzarella, cheeseburger filling or even fresh mango with coconut cheesecake filling.*

Makes 20 empanadas

Marinade and Pernil-Inspired Pork

4 cloves garlic

2 tbsp (6 g) fresh oregano leaves, about 2 sprigs or 1 tbsp (3 g) dried oregano

½ cup (8 g) loosely packed cilantro leaves, about 1 bunch, hard stems removed

1 tsp salt

1 tsp cumin

1 tsp fresh ground pepper

2 tbsp (30 ml) lime juice

1 tsp white vinegar

1 tbsp (15 ml) olive oil

2.2 lbs (1 kg) whole pork shoulder

Make the pork up to 4 days in advance by either using a slow cooker, which doesn't require marinating the pork and gives you a more hands-off approach, or by roasting the pork in the oven, which will give you a caramelized crust on the pork to mix into the meat. Once the pork is cooked, use two forks to shred the meat, or fit your stand mixer with the paddle attachment and mix on low speed for ease. Let the cooked, shredded pork cool to room temperature before transferring to an airtight container—it will be easier to mold your empanadas if the pork is not hot.

Option 1: Slow cook the pork. To make the marinade, blend the garlic, oregano, cilantro, salt, cumin, pepper, lime juice, vinegar and olive oil, then brush or rub it all over the pork shoulder. Place the pork inside the slow cooker, cover and cook for 6 to 8 hours on low until it shreds easily with a fork. I'd recommend letting it sit in the juices that develop in the slow cooker after you shred the meat for juicier pork.

(continued)

Empanada Dough (substitute with 20 frozen empanada discs)

4 cups (500 g) flour

1½ tsp (9 g) salt

½ tsp baking powder

1½ sticks (6 oz [170 g]) cold butter, cut into cubes (substitute with ¾ cup [144 g] vegetable shortening)

1 egg

⅓ cup (80 ml) ice-cold water, more as needed

Option 2: Roast the pork. First, marinate the pork by blending together the garlic, oregano, cilantro, salt, cumin, pepper, lime juice, vinegar and olive oil, then brush it all over the pork shoulder, getting into every crevice. Marinate in the refrigerator for at least 4 hours or overnight (if using) a bigger cut of pork than the recipe calls for. If roasting in the oven, remove from the fridge 1 hour before cooking to let it come back to room temperature for more even cooking. Preheat the oven to 275°F (135°C), then bake the pork with the fat cap up in a roasting pan or baking pan for 3 hours, or until the pork reaches an internal temperature of 160° F (70°C) and shreds easily with a fork.

Make the empanada dough. In a large bowl, combine the flour, salt and baking powder, then cut the cold butter into the flour using a pastry cutter or fork until you get a crumbly dough. You can also do this with a stand mixer with a dough hook or with a food processor—first mix/pulse the dry ingredients, then add the butter and mix or pulse until you get a crumbly dough. This process will create those morsels of fat that will stay solid in the dough and later melt when you fry or bake the empanadas to produce layers of flaky pastry.

Beat together the egg and ice-cold water, then gradually add to your crumbly dough and mix with your hands or the stand mixer/food processor until fully combined into a tacky dough, adding water as necessary to get all the flour incorporated.

Knead the dough on a clean work surface for 5 to 7 minutes or knead for a couple of minutes with the stand mixer or food processor, then place the ball of dough in a bowl covered with a silicon lid or plastic wrap and let the dough rest in the refrigerator for 30 minutes.

Cook the onion while the dough is resting. Heat 1 tablespoon (15 ml) of oil over medium heat in a skillet, then cook the onion for 6 to 8 minutes until softened and set aside to cool.

Make the plantains by heating the other half of the oil in the skillet over medium-high, then cook the plantains for 4 minutes per side until golden and caramelized. Set aside to cool.

Option 1: Roll out the dough and cut out empanada discs. Roll the empanada dough into a thin layer on a lightly floured working surface and use a cereal bowl to cut out perfect 6-inch (15-cm) circles from the dough, balling up and rolling out the scraps as needed to create about 20 empanada discs.

Option 2: Divide the dough and roll out each disc. Divide the dough into 20 balls—you can either weigh out the dough with a scale, or roll the dough into a long rope, eyeballing to cut equal-sized pieces. On a lightly floured working surface, roll out each ball into a thin circle about 6 inches (15 cm) in diameter, keeping the dough you are not working with covered.

Combine the empanada filling by mixing the shredded pork, onion and plantains until well combined, mashing the plantains into the filling. Scoop 1 to 2 tablespoons (8 to 16 g) of filling into the center of each empanada disc, then top with a small mound of cheese right in the center—this will give you a nice cheese-pull when you break them open. You want to pack as much filling into the empanadas as possible depending on the size of your disc.

Fold the empanadas into half-moons and lightly press the edges to seal first with your fingers. Press on the middle of the empanada and squeeze as much air out from the filling, press on the edges to seal again, then use a fork to crimp the edges. This will help really seal the edges and prevent the empanadas from exploding if air is trapped inside.

Cook the empanadas by either deep-frying (which will produce the crispiest, flakiest result), air frying or baking. To deep-fry, preheat a 1½-inch (4-cm) layer of oil in a Dutch oven or other high-walled pot over medium-high heat until 400°F (200°C), which will take 8 to 10 minutes. Fry the empanadas in the hot oil in batches, cooking for 4 to 5 minutes until golden brown, flipping as necessary and letting the oil come back up to temperature in between batches. To air fry, brush with egg wash and air fry at 400°F (200°C) for 8 to 12 minutes until golden brown. To bake, brush with egg wash and bake at 450°F (230°C) for 15 to 20 minutes until golden brown.

Make the green sauce by blending all the ingredients together until smooth, adding some or all of the jalapeño seeds to reach your desired heat level. You can make this up to 5 days in advance by storing in an airtight container. Transfer to a small bowl for dipping.

Serve the empanadas while hot, breaking them apart to show off the cheese-pull and let out the steam before dipping into your vibrant green sauce and digging in.

#CheesyPorkandPlantainEmpanadas #PocketsofLove
#IndulgentEatsatHome

Empanada Filling

2 tbsp (30 ml) olive oil, divided

1 medium onion, chopped

2–4 ripe plantains, sliced (depending on how sweet you want the empanadas)

1½–2 cups (170–226 g) shredded mozzarella cheese

Canola or vegetable oil, for frying

1–2 beaten eggs, optional

Spicy Green Sauce

3 jalapeños, seeds set aside

1 bunch cilantro, destemmed

2 cloves garlic

1 ripe avocado

¼ cup (56 g) mayo

1 tsp white vinegar

2 tsp (10 ml) fresh lime

½ tsp salt

1 tsp fresh ground pepper

3 tbsp (45 ml) olive oil

JUICY AF XIANBING
(Chinese Meat Pies)

Alexa, play Notorious B.I.G. because these Chinese meat pies are the definition of JUICY! They come out piping hot with a rich beef filling that pours out of a perfectly panfried, thin, crispy bun. Bing is a general term for Chinese flatbreads, pancakes and other doughy goods, and these flavorful versions hail from the northern city of Xi'an. I first tried them at Islam Food, a no-frills Hong Kong eatery that is famous for serving these halal meat pockets since 1950. My videos of them go viral every time, as the soup spilling out of that golden-brown pocket is the definition of drool-worthy (scan the QR code to watch!). It's the result of making aspic or gelatin made from meat broth—I'll dive into this technique more in the recipe.

While these are delicious with beef, you can actually make these with ground lamb or chicken, or go meatless by using Impossible plant-based meat—I tested it with great results! You can make the aspic as-is, or sub in vegetable broth to make these fully vegetarian.

Tip: Once you nail the technique, feel free to customize the filling. You could even stuff them with leftover Chicken Adobo (page 91) or Birria de Res (page 113) since the liquids will solidify enough when cold to use as filling. Let your imagination run wild!

Makes 8 meat pies

Aspic

1 medium-sized whole chicken or 3 chicken backs from the butcher (substitute with 1 cup [240 ml] of vegetable broth and ½ tsp agar agar powder for vegetarian version)

4 scallion greens, cut into thirds

6 slices ginger

Option 1: Make the aspic with chicken up to 2 days in advance. I'm borrowing a technique from an awesome Chinese food blog called Red House Spice that roasts a whole chicken to create a collagen-rich broth that will solidify into gelatin when it cools, which you can then stuff into the middle of your meat pies so it melts back to liquid when it's cooked.

Preheat the oven to 390°F (200°C). Stuff the inside of the chicken with the scallion greens and ginger, then bake the chicken in a Dutch oven or other large oven-safe pan with a tight-fitting lid for 1 hour. You can also use a roasting pan and cover everything tightly with aluminum foil. You want to trap the moisture inside so that as the collagen-rich liquid cooks out of the chicken it stays in the pan and doesn't evaporate, so really close it tight!

After 1 hour, remove from the oven and let it cool at room temperature while covered. Once the chicken is cool enough to handle with your hands, remove all the chicken from the bones to use in other recipes.

Optional: To make even more aspic so the buns are EXTRA juicy, you can roast the remaining bones in the same covered pan for another hour.

Transfer the liquid that develops in the bottom of the pan into an airtight container and let cool uncovered at room temperature before closing and transferring to the fridge.

(continued)

JUICY AF XIANBING (CONTINUED)

Dough

2 cups (250 g) all-purpose flour

Pinch of salt

⅓ cup (80 ml) hot water

¼ cup (60 ml) room temperature water, more as needed

1 tbsp (15 ml) vegetable cooking oil

Xianbing Filling

2 cloves garlic, minced

½ medium onion, chopped

1 bunch scallions, chopped

2 heaping tbsp (20 g) zha cai (pickled mustard tubers), minced, optional

8 oz (226 g) ground beef (substitute with ground lamb, chicken or Impossible plant-based meat)

1½ tbsp (22 ml) dark soy sauce

1–2 tsp (4–8 g) sugar

2 tsp (10 ml) oyster sauce

1 tsp Shaoxing wine

½ tsp sesame oil

½ tsp Chinese five spice powder

½ tsp white pepper

½–1 tsp cumin, optional

¼ tsp fresh ground Sichuan peppercorn, optional

1–2 tsp (2–4 g) chili flakes, optional

Tip: Use the juicy cooked chicken from making the aspic as a topping for Spicy Peanut Noods (page 48), a substitute for the lechon in Filipino Sizzling Pork Belly Sisig (page 111), extra protein for Arroz Caldo (page 167) or Jollof Rice (page 163) or for any meal prep needs. Plus, the rendered chicken fat (known as schmaltz) can be used in fried rice and for cooking vegetables for extra flavor.

Option 2: Make the vegetable broth gelatin. Bring the vegetable broth, agar agar, ginger and scallion greens to boil in a small saucepan, stirring to dissolve the powder. After 1 minute, turn off heat and discard the ginger and scallions. Let it cool enough so you can transfer to a container to store in the fridge until the gelatin has set, at least 30 minutes to an hour.

In a large bowl, make the dough by combining the flour and salt with a wooden spoon, then fully mix in the hot water followed by the room temperature water and oil until a rough dough forms. Turn the dough onto a clean working surface and knead for 5 to 7 minutes until a smooth ball forms. Cover and let it rest for at least 30 minutes.

In a medium bowl, make the filling by combining the garlic, onion, scallions, zha cai (if using), beef, soy sauce, sugar, oyster sauce, Shaoxing wine, sesame oil, five spice powder and pepper, along with the cumin, Sichuan peppercorn and chili flakes (if using). Use your hands to mix well. For easier prep, you can use a food processor to first pulse the roughly chopped garlic, ginger, onion, scallions and zha cai (if using) until minced, then add the meat and all the seasonings and pulse a few times until well combined, scraping down the sides throughout this process. Cook a spoonful of the meat in a skillet to taste for flavor and adjust the salt and other spices as desired. Set aside.

Prepare the gelatin. Scrape off the chicken fat that rose to the top of the container. You can store the rendered fat in an airtight container to use in place of oil—it will last up to 6 months in the freezer! Chop up the gelatin into tiny cubes and divide into eight equal portions, then set aside.

Divide the dough into eight equal-sized pieces. You can do this with a scale by measuring about 1.8 ounces (50 g) per piece, or by rolling the dough into a long rope. Cut the rope in half, then cut each half of the rope into four equal pieces so you have eight in total. Place a piece of dough on a lightly floured cutting board with the cut end facing up and press it into a flattened disc with your palm while you keep the rest of the dough covered so it doesn't dry out. Use a small rolling pin, wooden dowel or even a clean, tall unopened aluminum can (I use a soda water can) to then roll out the dough into a circle, rolling from the center out and rotating it as you go. This will take some practice but you'll get it eventually!

Scan the QR code to watch how I roll the dough and form the meat pies.

Option 1: Stuff and twist to form the meat pies. This is the easiest method. Make an OK symbol with your non-dominant hand, then use your dominant hand to place a disc of dough so the center is in line with the circle of your OK symbol. Now use your dominant hand to scoop 1 portion of aspic/gelatin followed by a heaping 2 tablespoons (about 40 to 50 g) of filling into the center, keeping your non-dominant hand in place while using your dominant hand thumb to push the filling into the dough and through the OK circle, continuing to press until it's fully enveloped with the dough. Then pinch together the ends to seal.

Option 2: Pleat like a dumpling. This is my preferred method for presentation. Keep the disc flat on your work surface, then add one portion of aspic/gelatin followed by a heaping 2 tablespoons (about 40 to 50 g) of filling to the center, making sure to keep the filling away from the ends. Now pick up one end of the dough disc and use your index fingers and thumbs to pinch and pleat the ends over the filling, toward the center to resemble a money bag or Nepali Momo (page 187)—try to flatten the pleats as you go to keep the dough thin. Twist the ends to make sure it's completely sealed. You want to stuff these so the wrapper is thin, but not so thin that the dough is translucent or else it might break when you panfry them. Feel free to use less filling to start as you practice forming the meat pies.

Panfry the meat pies. Heat 2 tablespoons (30 ml) of oil over medium heat. Place the meat pies with the pleated side down, pressing it into the oil to coat and into the pan to flatten—this will also really seal the pleated ends and help develop a nice crust. Cook until golden brown, 3 to 4 minutes, then use a spatula to carefully dig underneath (try not to touch the sides to avoid breaking the dough) to flip and cook another 3 to 4 minutes, adding oil as needed. Cover the pan and lower the heat to medium-low in the last 1 to 2 minutes of cooking, which will help steam the sides of the meat pies without burning the dough. Remove the lid and transfer to a paper towel–lined plate, using another paper towel to dab off any excess oil.

Wait a couple of minutes before eating as these are guaranteed to burn the crap out of your mouth! I usually bite a small hole on the top to let the steam escape and blow into the hole before sucking out a bit of soup and biting in. Get your napkins ready for the juicy explosion!

#JuicyAFXianbing #PocketsofLove #IndulgentEatsatHome

Frying
2–4 tbsp (30–60 ml) peanut, canola or vegetable oil

LAMB MASALA DUMPLINGS
with Cucumber Mint Raita

My favorite part about making dumplings is that you can recreate the flavors of your favorite dishes and put them into a perfect bite of goodness that you can always come back to weeks or months later. That's the magic behind these Lamb Masala Dumplings, which wrap up one of my favorite Indian dishes into little bundles that you can enjoy in as big or as small of a portion as you please. Because truthfully, my favorite part about Indian food is dipping freshly made, fluffy yet crispy naan into rich curries that have likely stewed for at least an hour. This is harder to recreate at home, from the time and experience needed to the equipment of a tandoor oven, so it's best saved for supporting your local Indian restaurants by dining in or ordering takeout and delivery when you can also eat the naan fresh. That's where these dumplings come in. I've done my best to infuse the flavors of lamb masala into these dumplings, which get panfried to mimic the crispy parts of naan.

Makes 40 to 50 dumplings

Cucumber Mint Raita

1 cup (227 g) Greek yogurt

¼ Hot House cucumber, grated

½ cup (43 g) fresh mint (about ½ bunch)

½ green chili, de-seeded and finely chopped, optional

Lamb Masala Filling

14 oz (397 g) ground lamb

8 tbsp (80 g) caramelized onions (page 220), chopped

1¼ tsp (3 g) garam masala

1–3 tsp (2–7 g) cayenne

1 tsp ground coriander

1 tsp smoked paprika

1 tsp cumin

1 tsp salt

1 clove garlic, minced

1 (1-inch [2.5-cm]) piece fresh ginger, minced

1 cup (96 g) loosely packed cilantro, chopped, plus more for garnish

Make the cucumber mint raita first so that the flavors have time to meld. In an airtight container, combine the yogurt, cucumber, mint and chili (if using) and store in the fridge while you pleat the dumplings, or in an airtight container for up to 3 days in advance.

In a medium bowl, make the filling by combining the lamb, onions, garam masala, cayenne, coriander, paprika, cumin, salt, garlic, ginger and cilantro. Use your hands to mix well. For easier prep, you can use a food processor to first pulse the caramelized onions, roughly chopped garlic and ginger and cilantro until minced; then add the lamb and all the seasonings and pulse a few times until well combined, scraping down the sides throughout this process. Cook a spoonful of the meat in a skillet to taste for flavor and adjust the salt and other spices as desired.

Prepare the dumpling folding area by placing the pile of dumpling wrappers on your work surface underneath a damp kitchen towel to prevent them from drying out. I like to put them on a big tray so I can also keep the folded dumplings under the damp towel. Place a small bowl of water nearby.

Scan the QR code to watch how to pleat and panfry these dumplings.

Option 1: Make an easy triangle pleat. Wet the edges of the wrapper, then add a spoonful of filling to the center. Pinch one end of the wrapper so it meets about a third of the way in, then use your opposite finger to press the opposite end toward the center so the two ends start to form the top of a triangle. Use your thumb to push the bottom in toward the center so that all three edges meet in the middle, forming a peace sign–like pattern. Press the edges to seal and shape the dumpling into a triangle.

(continued)

LAMB MASALA DUMPLINGS (CONTINUED)

Panfried Dumplings

50 dumpling wrappers, thawed, if frozen

2 tbsp (30 ml) canola or neutral oil

Quick Masala Dipping Sauce

1 tsp canola or vegetable oil

2 tbsp (34 g) tomato paste

2 tsp (5 g) garam masala

⅔ cup (160 ml) coconut milk

Salt and pepper, to taste

Option 2: Make a more advanced braided pleat. This is frankly easiest to learn by watching the video and practicing, but I'll do my best to write out instructions. Dip the edges of the wrapper in water, then add a spoonful of filling to the center of the wrapper and place it in your left hand or on a floured surface. Make four pleats on the right end of the wrapper with your right hand to form a pattern that looks like "WW," then press those pleats into the filling. Now use your index fingers to form a pleat that folds over the center from the right side and then another one from the left side to form your braided look. Continue pressing the center line of pleats into the filling, folding the wrapper from the right and then the left to form the braid all the way down. When you reach the end, pinch everything together (you can squeeze out any excess filling if there is any) and twist the end to seal it closed.

To panfry the dumplings, add the oil to a 9- or 10-inch (23- or 25-cm) nonstick or cast-iron skillet that has a lid, ideally a glass one so you can peek inside as they're cooking. Heat over medium-high, then once the oil is shimmering, add your dumplings to the pan by pressing each one into the oil, then moving it to form a circular pattern, starting from the outside ring and filling into the center. Panfry them for 1 to 2 minutes until the bottoms begin to turn golden brown.

Add water to the pan, then cover with the lid so that the steam cooks the inside and tops of the dumplings. Cook over medium-low heat for 5 minutes or until the dumpling wrappers look translucent. You can also use a slurry instead to create a crispy lattice—just follow the instructions on page 174 but skip adding the vinegar and sesame oil as directed. Transfer the cooked dumplings to a serving plate.

Start the quick masala dipping sauce while the dumplings are steaming so you can serve it hot. Heat the oil in a small saucepan over medium-high heat, then add the tomato paste and cook until brick red, about 5 minutes (you may need to plate the dumplings while this is cooking—don't worry, the sauce is forgiving!). Add the garam masala and the coconut milk, then stir together and simmer for a few minutes, tasting and adding salt and pepper as desired.

Serve the dumplings with chopped cilantro for garnish and the cucumber raita and masala dipping sauce on the side. Dip the dumplings into both for a perfect balance of rich and cooling flavors that also mimic the Indian flag colors 🇮🇳.

#LambMasalaDumplings #PocketsofLove #IndulgentEatsatHome

NEPALI MOMO
with Spicy Tomato Achar

Mo Money, Mo MOMOS! This type of dumpling can be found in the Himalayan region of Asia including Tibet (where it originated from), Bhutan, parts of India and finally, Nepal, which is the version that I will show you how to make. There's a big Nepali population in Hong Kong, resulting in plenty of establishments serving these juicy and flavorful steamed dumplings that are shaped either like half-moons like Chinese jiaozi or round pockets like xiao long bao, but with a big difference—tomato achar. This vibrant orange, addictively spicy roasted tomato-based chutney is what hooked me on momos, and what also sets apart the Nepali momos I've had in Hong Kong from the Tibetan versions found in NYC. The Lan Kwai Fong nightlife area of HK is famous for what I call #SecretMomos, as the unlicensed restaurant that serves them operates out of an old apartment. These are my way to honor the place that has saved me on many a drunken night.

Tip: *If you don't want to make your own dumpling wrappers, you can use store-bought wrappers and either pleat them into mini versions of momos or into half-moon shapes like my gyoza (page 172).*

Makes 16 to 22 momos

Spicy Tomato Achar

1 ripe tomato, halved

½—1 Thai bird's eye chili, stemmed, seeds set aside

1 (1½-inch [4-cm]) piece ginger

3 cloves garlic

¼ tsp fresh ground Sichuan peppercorn, optional

¼ tsp salt, plus more to taste

Momo Dough (substitute with 40–50 store-bought dumpling wrappers)

2½ cups (312 g) all-purpose flour, plus more as needed

¼ tsp salt

¾ cup (180 ml) hot water

1 tbsp (15 ml) canola or vegetable oil

Make the spicy tomato achar by first roasting the tomato in the oven at 400°F (200°C) for 30 minutes or in the air fryer at 400°F (200°C) for 15 minutes. Peel off the tomato skins, then blend the tomato, chili, ginger, garlic, peppercorn (if using) and salt until smooth; taste and add more salt or chili seeds to bring to your desired salt and heat level. Set aside to let the flavors mingle while you make the momos.

Make the momo dough by whisking together the flour and salt in a bowl until combined, then make a well in the center and add the water and oil, mixing the flour into the well of water until a shaggy dough mass forms. Turn the dough out onto a floured work surface and knead the dough for 5 to 7 minutes, adding flour, if needed, to form a barely tacky, smooth ball of dough. Alternatively, you can add the flour and salt to a stand mixer, let it run on medium-low with the dough hook while you slowly pour in the water and oil until a dough forms, then let it knead the dough for 4 to 5 minutes until smooth. Return the dough to the bowl, cover with a silicon lid or plastic wrap and let it rest for 30 minutes.

(continued)

Momo Filling

2 cloves garlic, minced

¼ red onion, finely chopped

½ cup (48 g) cilantro loosely packed, about 1 bunch, finely chopped

1 (1-inch [2.5-cm]) piece ginger, minced

12 oz (340 g) ground chicken thighs

1 tsp cumin

¼ tsp garam masala

¼ tsp nutmeg

1 tsp salt, plus more as needed

Pinch of fresh ground pepper

Steaming or Deep-Frying

Slices of cabbage, for steaming, optional

Canola or vegetable oil, for frying, optional

#NepaliMomo

#PocketsofLove

#IndulgentEatsatHome

Meanwhile, make the momo filling. In a large bowl, mix the garlic, onion, cilantro, ginger, chicken, cumin, garam masala, nutmeg, salt and pepper. For easier prep, you can add the roughly chopped garlic, red onion, cilantro and ginger to a food processor and pulse until finely chopped, then transfer to a large bowl. Use the food processor to grind the chicken thighs together with the spices and then combine that with everything else in the bowl. Cook a spoonful of the meat in a skillet to taste for seasoning and adjust the salt and other spices as desired. Cover and store in the fridge until ready to use.

Divide the dough into 16 to 22 equal-sized balls (about 0.9 to 1 ounce [25 to 30 g] in weight). Keep the rest of the dough covered while you roll out each wrapper on a lightly floured working surface, first using your hand to flatten the ball into a disc, then rolling the dough out into a thin 4-inch (10-cm)-wide circle so it's thinner on the ends.

Pleat the momo into half-moons like gyoza (page 172) or similar to xiao long bao. First add a heaping spoonful of filling to the center. Place the dumpling in your non-dominant hand, then pinch the dough with your dominant hand to make a pleat. Now keep your non-dominant hand thumb in place, tucking the filling into the dough while using your index finger and your dominant hand thumb to continue pleating the dough, going around in a circle until you've pleated it all the way around. When you get to the end, twist the ends together to seal. Keep the pleated momo on a tray lightly greased with oil and covered with a damp kitchen towel so they don't dry out.

Option 1: Steam the momo. This is the most traditional preparation. You will need either a steamer basket (bamboo steamer baskets work best) or a ceramic plate that can sit on top of an upside down ceramic bowl that fits inside a wok or pot with a lid. Line the steamer basket or plate with a piece of parchment paper or a slice of cabbage, which will prevent the dumplings from sticking. Add as many dumplings as can fit without them touching inside the steamer—you will have to cook them in batches. Add a little more than 1 inch (2.5 cm) of water to the bottom of a wok or pot (along with the upside down bowl), then bring to a boil over high heat. Once there is steam, reduce the heat to medium and add the steamer basket or plate, close the lid and steam for 9 to 12 minutes until the dumpling skins are slightly translucent.

Option 2: Deep-fry the momo. Heat a 2-inch (5-cm) depth of oil in a Dutch oven or small pot to 350°F (180°C), then deep-fry the dumplings for 2 to 3 minutes until golden brown. Transfer to a paper towel–lined plate and dab excess oil.

Serve the momo with tomato achar and enjoy immediately.

JAMAICAN BEEF PATTIES

With juicy, uniquely spiced ground beef encased in a flaky dough, Jamaican beef patties are perfect pockets of goodness that immediately transport me back to the islands. While I grew up eating mass-produced beef patties, like those you can find frozen from Costco or at pizza places in NYC (which were still so satisfying), I had the pleasure of trying the best versions during a media trip to Jamaica in 2017. It was one of my favorite media trips I've ever been on thanks to my guides from the tourism board, who took me and my husband beyond the well-known island resort areas to explore the capital city of Kingston.

Not only did we try Jamaica's famous Blue Mountain coffee and local street food like pan chicken, but we taste-tested four beef patty spots, including local institution Devon House and popular chains Tastee and Juici. While there were a lot of differences between the patties, a few things were consistent: a molten, spicy beef filling and a crispy, supremely flaky dough that left crumbs all over. After rounds of recipe testing, these patties check all the boxes! So, play your favorite reggae tunes while you knead and roll your way into tasty, juicy beef patty heaven.

Makes 12 large patties or 20 small patties
(6 large or 10 small patties if only making half the recipe)

Jamaican Beef Patty Filling

2 tbsp (28 g) unsalted butter

2 tbsp (30 ml) olive oil

1 medium yellow onion, finely chopped

3 cloves garlic, minced

1 lb (454 g) ground beef or Impossible plant-based meat

½–1 Scotch bonnet pepper, habanero pepper or 1–2 tbsp (15–30 ml) Scotch bonnet hot sauce

2 tsp (4 g) paprika

1 tsp black pepper, plus more to taste

1½ tsp (3 g) dried thyme

¾ tsp allspice

1 tsp soy sauce

½ tsp ground coriander

½ beef bouillon cube

2 cups (480 ml) water

½ cup (54 g) bread crumbs

Salt, to taste

First let's cook the onion for the beef patty filling. Melt the butter with the olive oil over medium-low heat, then add the onion and cook while stirring occasionally until soft and translucent, about 5 minutes. Stir in the garlic and cook until aromatic, about another minute.

Add the ground beef and raise the heat to medium-high. Brown the meat for 8 to 10 minutes, using a wooden spoon to break it up into tiny pieces and stir for even browning.

Add all the spices, including the beef bouillon cube, breaking up the cube with the wooden spoon, stirring until everything is well combined and sautéing for another minute before adding the water. Bring to a boil, then simmer on medium-low heat for 15 to 20 minutes uncovered until most of the liquid has been absorbed except a thin layer of liquid on the bottom of the pan. This will help tenderize the ground beef.

Mix in the bread crumbs and allow them to absorb the remaining liquid so none of that flavor gets lost! Add salt and pepper to taste, then set this aside to cool while you make the dough or refrigerate for up to 3 to 4 days to make ahead of time.

(continued)

Pastry Dough

3½ cups (438 g) all-purpose flour

1 tsp salt

1 tsp granulated sugar

1 tbsp (7 g) turmeric

3.5 oz (99 g) beef suet or tallow, frozen and chopped into cubes then frozen again (substitute with ½ cup [120 g] cold butter, cut into cubes then put back in the refrigerator)

1 cup (240 ml) ice-cold water

Make the pastry dough by cutting the beef fat or butter into the flour. You can do this by mixing together the flour, salt, sugar, turmeric, beef suet or tallow and water in a standing mixer with a dough hook, in a food processor or in a large bowl with a pastry cutter. This will create those morsels of fat that will stay solid in the dough and later melt during baking to produce layers of flaky pastry. Once the fat and flour are combined into a crumbly dough, add the ice-cold water and mix until fully combined, using your hands to knead the dough as necessary to get all the flour incorporated. Form a ball with the dough, then cover the bowl with a silicon lid or wrap the dough in plastic wrap and let the dough rest in the refrigerator for 30 minutes.

Divide the dough into even portions using a knife or bench scraper and a scale if you have one. Bigger patties need about 4 ounces (72 g) of dough, while smaller ones need about 2 ounces (48 g) of dough. I like to split the dough in half and make six big ones and ten small ones. If you don't have a scale, you can eyeball it by rolling the dough into two long, equal-sized logs, and then cutting each log into either six or ten even pieces.

Preheat the oven to 400°F (200°C) so it's ready to go after you've folded your first round of patties, this way you'll have some ready to eat by the time you're done rolling out and folding all the patties. Prepare one or two baking trays with parchment paper to place the folded patties onto.

Roll out the dough into a long, symmetrical, rounded rectangle, working one at a time on a lightly floured working surface. Then spoon 1½ tablespoons (13 g) of filling for the small patties and 3 tablespoons (26 g) for the big patties onto one side of the dough. Fold the other side over so the ends meet and use a fork to press the edges together. Place the completed patties onto the baking trays with a bit of space in between.

Bake for 20 to 25 minutes or air fry for 12 to 14 minutes until golden brown and crispy on the outside. Let them sit for a few minutes when they come out of the oven before breaking in to see those beautiful layers and let the steam escape so you can bite into that perfectly flaky, spicy, meaty pocket of love.

#JamaicanBeefPatties #PocketsofLove #IndulgentEatsatHome

SINGAPORE CHILI CRAB RANGOON

These crazy rich wontons are my mash-up of one of the most iconic dishes of Singapore with a uniquely Americanized Chinese dish with vague Burmese origins (as Rangoon is the name of the former capital of Burma/Myanmar). While cream cheese is certainly not typical in Southeast Asian cuisine, I absolutely love crab rangoon in all their unabashed inauthenticity, as this product of immigration had a firm place in my immigrant family's weekend takeout menu order. I wanted to put my spin on these deep-fried imitation crab and cream cheese wontons by replacing the sauce with one inspired by Singapore chili crab.

While you should make your way to Singapore (or restaurants like Laut in NYC) to try the real deal crabs stir-fried in a thick tomato, chili and egg gravy, you can consider these dumplings a gateway to those flavors without the mess of breaking open a sauce-covered crab by hand. Since cream cheese has a very strong flavor, feel free to save some money by using imitation crab in the crab rangoon or use real crab meat and make these without the cream cheese if you'd prefer that the overall taste be closer to the traditional Singapore chili crab flavor.

Makes 20 crab rangoon

Crab Rangoon Filling

8 oz (226 g) cream cheese, softened, optional (halve the rest of the ingredients if omitting)

2 cloves garlic, grated

1 (1-inch [2.5-cm]) piece ginger, peeled and grated

4 stalks scallions, chopped

¼ cup (24 g) loosely packed fresh cilantro (about ½ bunch), chopped

½ tsp white pepper

¼ tsp Worcestershire sauce

¼ tsp sesame oil

4 oz (113 g) crab meat or imitation crab

Crab Rangoon Assembly

20 wonton wrappers

½ egg, beaten (use the rest in the dipping sauce)

Canola or vegetable oil, for frying

In a medium bowl, make the filling by combining the cream cheese (if using), garlic, ginger, scallions, cilantro, pepper, Worcestershire sauce, sesame oil and crab. For easier prep, you can use a food processor to first pulse the garlic, ginger, scallions and cilantro until minced, then combine them well in a bowl with the remaining ingredients.

Prepare a crab rangoon assembly area by placing the pile of wonton wrappers on your work surface underneath a damp kitchen towel to prevent them from drying out. I like to put them on a big tray so I can also keep the folded wontons under the damp towel. Beat the egg in a small bowl and place it nearby.

Fold the crab rangoon. There are four popular methods for doing this depending on difficulty and presentation—scan the QR code to watch how its done. Regardless of the method, you first need to wet the edges of the wrapper with the beaten egg, then add a teaspoon of filling to the center of the wrapper. You don't want to add any more or your crab rangoon will likely explode no matter how much you squeeze out the air. This is because cream cheese has a lot of moisture, which turns into steam in the hot oil, and too much steam will literally inflate the inside of the wrapper like a balloon until it finally pops and explodes (I know from experience 😩).

(continued)

Singapore Chili Crab Dipping Sauce (substitute with sweet chili sauce or gyoza dipping sauce [page 175])

½ tbsp (7 ml) canola or vegetable oil

½ shallot, minced

1 clove garlic, minced

1 (½-inch [1.3-cm]) piece ginger, minced or grated

1 Thai bird's eye chili, chopped, seeds set aside

2 tbsp (30 ml) ketchup

4 tbsp (60 ml) sweet chili sauce

½ egg, beaten

Salt to taste

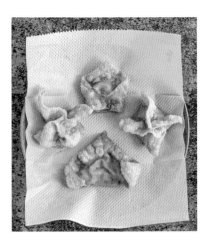

#SingaporeChiliCrabRangoon

#PocketsofLove

#IndulgentEatsatHome

Option 1: The Flower. This is the most difficult, but my preferred method for folding crab rangoon because it forces you to use less filling and results in a high ratio of crispy edges to creamy filling—plus, they're pretty! Pinch opposite straight ends of the wrapper together to meet in the middle, then pinch the other opposite ends toward the center, to form an "X" in the center. Squeeze out the air as you press all the edges along the "X" to seal in the filling.

Option 2: The Square. This is basically the reverse of The Flower, where you form a "+" instead of an "X". Bring the top two corners toward the center to form a triangle shape on top, sealing along the edges that are touching, then bring the bottom corners up to the middle so the edges form a "+" sign. Squeeze out the air before sealing all the edges.

Option 3: The Triangle. The easiest method of them all—just fold the wrapper in half diagonally and have the ends meet to form a triangle. If you want to make big crab rangoon, you can use egg roll wrappers, which are sturdier than wonton wrappers and less likely to explode so you can use a spoonful or more of filling to turn them into big triangles.

Option 4: The Envelope. Take your Triangle, and simply fold the two end corners into the center, using egg wash to seal so it looks like an open envelope.

Freeze the crab rangoon on a parchment paper–lined tray for 30 minutes to help prevent explosions, since it will allow the outside to fry before the cream cheese gets too hot to start steaming.

Heat the frying oil for 5 to 10 minutes before you take the crab rangoon out of the freezer. Heat a 2-inch (5-cm) depth of oil in a Dutch oven or small pot to 350°F (180°C).

Make the Singapore chili crab dipping sauce right after you start heating the oil for frying. Heat the oil in a small nonstick skillet over medium heat, then add the shallot and cook until softened, about 3 minutes. Add the garlic, ginger and bird's eye chili and cook until fragrant, another minute. Add the ketchup and sweet chili sauce and bring to a simmer, then drizzle in the beaten egg. Let it sit for a minute before swirling the egg into the sauce so you form small curds. Taste, add salt and chili seeds as desired, then turn off the heat and set aside.

Deep-fry the crab rangoon for 2 to 3 minutes until golden brown. Transfer to a paper towel–lined plate and dab up the excess oil.

Serve the crab rangoon with the Singapore chili crab dipping sauce.

Sweet Tooth

Truthfully, I never thought of myself as having a sweet tooth. For most of my adult life, I wouldn't even look at the dessert menu at a restaurant, let alone order from it. If someone else ordered dessert for the table, I'd have only one or two bites just to try it. I always shared my ice cream, and regularly finished meals that DID include dessert with something savory (like a last bite of fries or a cheese course). That being said, there were several categories of dessert that were MASSIVE exceptions to this behavior: Filipino, cheesecake, matcha, mango, salty-sweet and dark chocolate (I'd eat a square after almost every meal, healthy ones included). So, it should come as no surprise that these tastes dictated the recipes you'll find in this section of the cookbook.

Filipino desserts started taking Instagram by storm in recent years as the world feasted their eyes on *ube* (pronounced oo-beh), a delicious, vibrant purple yam native to the Philippines—flip to the next page for a full explainer. Here I'm using ube in both a Filipino-meets-French mille-feuille (page 201) that layers an ube coconut cheesecake cream between layers of crispy, flaky puff pastry, and in a showstopping leche flan–topped ube cake (page 203) that combines two popular Filipino desserts into one. Both desserts can also be made without ube if you have trouble sourcing it or aren't as big of a fan of the flavor.

I've also included another Filipino dessert called Mango Float (page 215), and a strawberry-topped Matcha Pavlova (page 211) to satisfy those who prefer fruit-filled sweets. The pavlova is also the perfect way to use up all the leftover egg whites you're bound to have in making this cookbook. And for my fellow sweet-and-salty dessert lovers, my Levain Bakery–style giant gooey cookies take the flavor of dark chocolate–covered potato chips and turn it into the most decadent and satisfying cookie ever (page 207). They were so good that I couldn't help eating at least one whole cookie from every batch of recipe testing. Maybe I do have a sweet tooth after all. . . .

WHAT THE HECK IS UBE?

Ube (pronounced oo-beh) is a purple yam native to the Philippines and other Southeast Asian countries. It has a very unique flavor that's hard to describe without tasting it, but I think of it as vanilla with subtle hints of pistachio, sweet potato and taro—another purple root vegetable that it's often mistaken for. Ube is near and dear to my heart, as I grew up scooping spoonfuls of ube halaya into my mouth, savoring the thick, creamy jam that's made by cooking mashed ube with milk and butter.

Sourcing good ube halaya will make a huge impact in how delicious your desserts are. It's best found freshly made at Filipino markets and restaurants. The jarred versions available in markets and online are the next best option, though the flavor you get when ube halaya is freshly made is unparalleled. If you have the time and can find fresh or frozen ube, it's worth making your own ube halaya. You can find recipes for this online, including on my site by scanning the QR code in the corner of this page. You can then use the ube halaya for making the next two desserts in this book, as well as in cheesecake, crinkle cookies, butter mochi, ice cream or enjoying it straight out of the jar.

UBE COCONUT CHEESECAKE MILLE-FEUILLE

ASMR never looked prettier. The classic French pastry mille-feuille (pronounced meal-FOY-uh) translates to "thousand sheets," with those endless layers of puff pastry combining with pastry cream to produce one of my absolute favorite sweet treats. I can't help but order it if it's on a dessert menu, so I wanted to present my version with a vibrant purple ube coconut cheesecake cream to bring in my Filipino roots. You can easily substitute the ube for mashed fruit or matcha or even omit any add-ins to change the flavor. By using store-bought puff pastry, what might be a laborious dessert comes together in as quickly as 15 minutes.

Makes 2 to 4 servings

4 oz (113 g) cream cheese, room temperature

4 tbsp (55 g) ube halaya, room temperature (substitute with an additional 1 oz [28 g] cream cheese or your choice of mashed fruit or fruit jam)

½ cup (120 ml) coconut cream or coconut milk (substitute with whipping cream that's been whipped to a thick consistency, see recipe for details)

1 square sheet puff pastry, thawed, if frozen

¼ tsp ube extract (use ½ tsp if omitting the ube halaya and want to maintain the ube flavor, substitute with other flavor extract or 1–2 tsp [2–4 g] matcha)

¼ tsp vanilla extract

2 tsp (8 g) caster sugar, plus more to taste (substitute with granulated sugar)

1 tbsp (12 g) granulated sugar

1–2 tbsp (7–15 g) powdered sugar, for garnish

Prepare the ingredients. Bring the cream cheese and ube halaya to room temperature by removing them from the refrigerator 1 hour before making the dessert. If you're using coconut milk, now is a good time to stick that in the fridge. It will thicken up to be closer consistency to coconut cream, since we want it THICC to produce a mousse-like texture for the final cheesecake cream. Fifteen minutes before making the dessert, let the frozen puff pastry sit flat on a cutting board to thaw.

Preheat the oven to 400°F (200°C) and line a baking sheet with parchment paper or a silicon mat.

Make the ube coconut cheesecake cream. First, combine the coconut cream or the coconut milk (scoop it out with a spoon, discarding the water left in the bottom of the can) with the ube extract and/or vanilla extract and the caster sugar in a large bowl or the bowl of a stand mixer. Whip over medium-high speed with an electric mixer or a stand mixer until well combined, which should only take several seconds. If you are using whipping cream, whisk until medium peaks form, 1 to 2 minutes. Then, add the cream cheese and ube halaya or your choice substitution, and whip until fully combined, scraping down the sides of the bowl as needed with a rubber spatula. Taste the mixture and mix in more caster sugar as needed, whisking it well so the sugar dissolves.

For a prettier presentation, transfer the mixture to a piping bag fixed with a nozzle. You can also put it in a sandwich bag and just cut off the tip of the bag when it's time to pipe the cream, or leave the mixture in the bowl to simply spread onto the puff pastry later. Whichever you do, make sure to transfer the piping bag, sandwich bag or bowl to the fridge for at least 15 minutes so the cream can stiffen up.

Optional: Roll out the puff pastry so it's a bit thinner—this will help the texture but isn't necessary if you want to save time.

(continued)

Poke holes all over the puff pastry with a fork. You want the holes to be uniformly distributed all over, so keep poking! This will prevent it from puffing too much and keep it flat. Sprinkle granulated sugar evenly over the top, then transfer to the baking sheet.

Bake the puff pastry for 12 to 15 minutes until golden brown and crispy, then remove it from the oven and let it cool on a wire rack.

Milles-feuille ASSEMBLE! Use a serrated knife to GENTLY cut off all the ends of the puff pastry to reveal those beautiful layers, working in tiny strokes to minimize damage to the puff pastry. Then, cut the square into thirds so you have three equal-sized long rectangles—use a ruler if necessary. Now pipe the cheesecake cream onto two of the rectangles, making little dollops of cheesecake cream in two or three rows, depending on how you want it to look. For ease, you can also pipe the cream into two to three long rows, or just skip the piping bag and spread the cream on with a knife—it's really up to you! Once you've covered two of the rectangles with cream, stack the puff pastry rectangles onto one another so you have one long mille-feuille.

Refrigerate the mille-feuille for at least 2 hours, which will help everything set and stay stuck together while miraculously staying crispy, though you can certainly eat it right after assembling if you don't want to wait. If you plan to keep it in the fridge for longer, transfer it to an airtight container, which should keep it crispy for up to 6 hours from my experience. When it's ready to serve, dust with powdered sugar as desired, use a serrated knife to gently slice it and enjoy!

#UbeMilleFeuille #SweetTooth #IndulgentEatsatHome

UBE LECHE FLAN CAKE

"Whoa what is THAT?!" is the reaction you're bound to get to this stunning cake. It's Filipino dessert heaven, as it stacks bright purple ube cake together with the creamy, caramel-topped custard of leche flan, inspired by the viral ube leche flan cupcakes from West Coast bakery, Cafe 86. You can also make the leche flan to enjoy on its own, as a topping for ice cream and shaved ice like the Filipino dessert halo-halo or cover the ube cake with vanilla frosting and toasted coconut for a more traditional cake.

Want to take it to the next level? Make a marbled cake by turning half of the batter into either a coconut or cheddar cheese chiffon cake batter. And yes, I said CHEDDAR cheese! Ube and cheese is a delicious flavor pairing that's popular in the Philippines as an ice cream flavor and in a viral pastry called ube cheese pandesal. Give the cheese a try to add just the right level of savoriness to this sweet cake or go more tropical with coconut cake.

Makes a four-layer cake using two 6-inch (15-cm) cake pans or a two-layer cake using one 9-inch (23-cm) cake pan

Leche Flan

½–1 cup (100–200 g) sugar, depending on preferred level of sweetness

2 tbsp (30 ml) water

⅛ tsp cream of tartar or ¼ tsp lemon juice

8 egg yolks

1 cup (240 ml) evaporated milk

¾–1 cup (180–240 ml) condensed milk, depending on preferred level of sweetness

¼ tsp vanilla extract

Preheat the oven to 350°F (180°C). We will be baking the cakes in a water bath to keep the leche flan custardy, so you will need a high-walled baking pan that will fit your cake pan(s).

Make the caramel by whisking the sugar and water in a nonstick pan over medium heat until fully dissolved. Mix in the cream of tartar or lemon juice to help stabilize the caramel. Cook over medium heat without stirring until it turns into a light caramel color, 6 to 8 minutes. Remove from the heat and distribute evenly into the cake pan(s). Swirl the pan(s) to coat in an even layer of caramel, then set aside.

In a small bowl, whisk together the egg yolks, evaporated and condensed milks and vanilla until well combined, but do it gently to try not to make bubbles. Distribute it evenly between the cake pan(s), pouring it through a mesh strainer to remove anything that didn't fully dissolve.

(continued)

Ube Chiffon Cake Batter

4 egg yolks

4 tbsp (48 g) sugar

4 tbsp (55 g) ube halaya (substitute with 1 tsp ube extract, for a total of 2 tsp [10 ml])

1 tsp ube extract

½ tsp vanilla extract

2 drops purple food coloring, optional

4 tbsp (60 ml) milk

4 tbsp (60 ml) canola or vegetable oil

1 cup (125 g) cake flour

1½ tsp (7 g) baking powder

½ tsp salt

Cheese or Coconut Chiffon Cake Batter (optional—halve the ube batter ingredients if making)

2 egg yolks

2 tbsp (24 g) sugar

½ cup (57 g) shredded cheddar cheese (if making cheese chiffon cake)

¼ tsp vanilla extract

2 tbsp (30 ml) milk (or coconut milk if making coconut chiffon cake)

2 tbsp (30 ml) canola or vegetable oil

½ cup (63 g) cake flour

¾ tsp baking powder

¼ tsp salt

Egg White Meringue

4 egg whites

¼ tsp cream of tartar or ½ tsp lemon juice

¼ cup (48 g) sugar

If you are making a marbled cake, complete the following steps in two separate mixing bowls—one for your ube cake batter and one for the coconut or cheese cake batter. It will require double the bowls, whisks and spatulas and almost double the work since you need to make two cake batters, but it's worth giving it a try if you've already succeeded in making this cake and want to level up. **Otherwise,** just follow the next steps as listed.

Make the cake batter. Whisk the egg yolks and sugar until lighter in color and frothy, 1 to 2 minutes depending on how fast you whisk.

Add the ube halaya to the ube cake batter (if using), mashing it into the egg as much as possible to remove any lumps. Add the cheddar cheese to the cheese cake batter (if using).

Add the ube extract (for the ube cake batter), vanilla extract, food coloring (for the ube cake batter, if using), milk (or coconut milk) and oil. Whisk until fully combined.

Sift in the flour and baking powder, then use a whisk to mix it in along with the salt until just combined. Be sure to scrape up the bottom and down the sides of the bowl for a uniform batter and try to remove any lumps with the whisk as you're mixing, but don't overmix or your cake won't be fluffy. Set aside.

Make the egg white meringue. Beat the egg whites on the highest speed until foamy, then add the cream of tartar and continue beating until the egg whites become opaque white. Then, gradually add in the sugar and beat until stiff peaks form, which should take a total of 2 to 3 minutes from when you started beating them—check this by lifting up the beater to see if the egg whites stand right up with stiff peaks that bend over slightly.

Fold the meringue into the cake batter(s). Use a rubber spatula to scoop a third of the meringue into the batter at a time (if making a marbled cake, add a sixth into each batter at a time so that you evenly divide the meringue between the two cake batters), gently scooping from the bottom and folding the batter onto itself until there are no more white streaks, turning the bowl as necessary. Do this again with another third (or sixth) of the batter, making sure to stay gentle as you don't want the meringue to deflate. Once that's incorporated, add the remaining meringue and gently fold until there are no more white streaks.

Boil 3 to 4 cups (720 ml to 1 L) of water; you need enough to fill the baking pan halfway for the water bath. It works best if you use a tea kettle with a long spout.

(continued)

UBE LECHE FLAN CAKE (CONTINUED)

Divide the cake batter evenly into the cake pans, distributing as evenly across the top of the leche flan as possible and making sure to leave ¼ inch (6 mm) of space below the rim since the cake will rise. If you have any leftover batter, you can save it to bake cupcakes.

If making a marbled cake, add two to three large scoopfuls of ube cake batter to the center of each pan first, then add two to three large scoopfuls of coconut/cheese cake batter to the center, and continue alternating to create thick concentric circles of the two cake batters until you use all of the batter. If desired, you can then use a knife to run through the batter and make swirls.

Pick up and drop the cake pans on the counter several times to knock out any big air bubbles in the batter.

Bake for 25 to 30 minutes, until the top of the cake looks dry. Then, carefully remove just the smaller cake pan (NOT the baking pan filled with the water bath) from the oven. It's incredibly important that you keep the water bath stable and level during this part. I had a bad accident where I burned myself accidentally spilling the water bath, so PLEASE be extra careful and wear an apron and long oven mitts when doing this process! Once you have the cake pan(s) out of the oven, carefully cover the top(s) with aluminum foil to prevent them from burning, then gently place it back into the center of the water bath.

Continue baking for 25 to 30 minutes, until a toothpick inserted in the center comes out clean. Remove the cakes from the water bath and let them cool to room temperature, then transfer the cakes to the fridge to chill for at least 2 hours to let the leche flan set.

The big reveal! Use a butter knife to run around the edges of the cake to loosen it from the pan. Place a cake stand or serving plate upside down onto the opening of the cake pan, then carefully but confidently flip the entire thing over. Jiggle and tap on the pan as needed to let the ube leche flan cake drop and lift it up to let the liquified caramel flow all over the cake. Do this in front of your guests and make sure someone is filming for a big "OOOHH, AHHH" moment. But the fun isn't over if you used 6-inch (15-cm) cake pans! Carefully but confidently flip the next ube leche flan cake layer on top, using the cake pan to line the layers up, then tap on the pan and jiggle to lift off the cake pan and reveal the second cake. Take a bow for your cake flipping skills, then cut out a slice to show off those beautiful layers once more and enjoy all the decadent flavors and textures of this ube leche flan cake.

#UbeLecheFlan #SweetTooth #IndulgentEatsatHome

GIANT GOOEY POTATO CHIP-DARK CHOCOLATE CHEESECAKE COOKIES

If you're a fan of sea salt–studded dark chocolate or have ever experienced the salty-sweet dream that is potato chips dipped in dark chocolate, then this is the cookie for you. It's big and gooey in the center, based on the world-famous chocolate chip walnut cookies from Levain Bakery in New York. I'm using potato chips instead of walnuts to add a more delicate crispy texture and to add a subtle saltiness to the endless tiny pockets of melted dark chocolate (though you can sub in semisweet or even peanut butter chips to adjust the sweetness and flavor).

For extra indulgence, stuff them with a tangy creamy cheesecake filling that slowly pulls apart when you break them open. Finish the cookies with a sprinkle of flaky sea salt to really drive the salty-sweet flavors or leave it out along with the potato chips to make this a more classic double chocolate cookie. Alternatively, you can even leave out the cocoa in the cookie dough to make regular chocolate chip cookies—it's easy to customize the dough once you have the general formula to create the giant gooey cookie of your dreams.

Makes 8 to 12 cookies

Cheesecake Filling (optional)

4 oz (113 g) cream cheese, softened

¼ cup (30 g) powdered or confectioners' sugar, more to taste

¼ tsp vanilla extract

Giant Gooey Cookie Dough

8 oz (226 g) cold butter, cut into small cubes

1 cup (200 g) brown sugar

½ cup (100 g) granulated sugar

2 eggs

1½ cups (188 g) all-purpose flour

1 cup (125 g) cake flour

½ cup (32 g) baking cocoa (substitute with cake flour for regular chocolate chip cookies)

1 tsp cornstarch

¾ tsp baking soda

½ tsp salt

Make the cheesecake filling (if using). Beat together the cream cheese, sugar and vanilla extract in a large bowl with an electric mixer or in a stand mixer on medium-high speed until smooth and creamy, about 3 minutes. Divide the filling into 8 to 12 spoonfuls (depending on how many cookies you're making) in a silicon ice cube tray (I love using my Souper Cubes® for this) or on a lined baking sheet or tray that will fit in your freezer. Freeze for 1 to 2 hours until solidified or up to 2 to 3 days in advance.

Get the oven hot and the butter cold. Preheat the oven to 410°F (210°C), as you want to bake the cookies at high heat for a short amount of time so that the outside gets crisp quickly while the inside stays gooey. You can also use your air fryer instead, which I prefer since it gets the potato chips golden brown. If you are air frying, you don't have to preheat the air fryer until a few minutes before baking. However, you want to make sure the butter is cold. After you cut it into small cubes, put it back in the fridge while you gather the rest of the ingredients.

In a stand mixer fitted with a paddle attachment, cream together the cold butter, brown sugar and granulated sugar on high speed until the color becomes lighter and the texture is fluffy, about 4 minutes. Add an egg and mix on low until combined, then add the second egg and mix well again. Add the all-purpose flour, cake flour, baking cocoa, cornstarch, baking soda and salt. Stir until fully combined, scraping down the sides of the bowl as needed, but be sure not to overmix or your cookies will end up being flatter when they bake.

(continued)

GIANT GOOEY POTATO CHIP-DARK CHOCOLATE CHEESECAKE COOKIES (CONTINUED)

Cookie Dough Mix-Ins

¾ cup (168 g) roughly chopped dark chocolate from a bar (I like using at least 75% cocoa chocolate to reduce the sugar; substitute with your choice of chocolate bar)

¼–½ cup (60–120 g) dark chocolate chips (substitute with semisweet, white chocolate or peanut butter chips)

1–2 cups (32–64 g) Ruffles® or other ridged potato chips, gently crushed (substitute with toasted nuts, pretzels, crispy bacon or other mix-ins)

Flaky sea salt (like Maldon®), to taste

Gently fold in your preferred mix-ins. I like to reserve a handful of the mix-ins to press on top of the cookie for presentation, and to add a crispier texture since the potato chips will not be quite as crispy after they're mixed into the cookie dough, but you're welcome to also just mix everything all at once.

Divide and roll the cookie dough into giant balls. I like to go big or go home and make eight giant cookies. You can either use a scale to divide even portions, use an ice cream scoop or just eyeball it. Use your hands to roll them into balls. If you are stuffing them with the cheesecake filling, roll the frozen spoonfuls of cream cheese into balls, make a deep hole into the middle of each ball of cookie dough, stuff the ball of cheesecake filling inside, wrap the cookie dough around it and roll it to seal.

Press any reserved mix-ins and a sprinkle of flaky sea salt on the tops of the cookies—an easy way to do this is to combine the mix-ins in a bowl and roll the top of the cookie dough ball in the bowl.

Stick the balls of dough in the fridge for at least 30 minutes—the shape will hold even better if you can chill them for a few hours or overnight in an airtight container. You can also make the dough ahead of time and store it for up to 3 days in the fridge or 3 months in the freezer.

If you are using the air fryer, preheat the air fryer to 400ºF (200ºC) for at least 3 to 5 minutes.

(continued)

GIANT GOOEY POTATO CHIP-DARK CHOCOLATE CHEESECAKE COOKIES (CONTINUED)

Arrange the balls of cookie dough on a silicon mat or parchment paper that fits on a baking sheet or in your air fryer basket (so that's four to six cookies per baking sheet or two to four cookies depending on the size of your air fryer basket) and spaced 2 inches (5 cm) apart. If using the air fryer, I find that it's easiest to keep each cookie on its own smaller piece of parchment paper so you can lift each one out without them smashing into one another.

Bake for 11 to 18 minutes or air fry for 7 to 14 minutes, depending on the size of the balls and how chilled or frozen they are, until the exterior is solid and crisp. For example, the cookies pictured came from a batch of eight, and were air fried for 11 minutes out of the refrigerator. They might seem underbaked inside, but they just need time to set and the residual heat will make sure the center is cooked but still gooey. You can also bake them for longer based on how sturdy you want the cookies to be. Remove them from the oven or air fryer (I like to lift opposite edges of the parchment paper to remove them from the air fryer basket since the cookies will be very soft).

Let them cool on the parchment paper on a wire rack for at least 10 to 15 minutes. If the cookies are spreading flat, you can use clean hands or a spoon to push the sides in while they are cooling since the shape will hold as the cookies cool.

Break open the cookies to reveal that gooey center and enjoy with a cold glass of milk or a scoop of vanilla ice cream on the side.

#GiantGooeyCookies #SweetTooth #IndulgentEatsatHome

MATCHA PAVLOVA
with Strawberries and Salted Caramel

Sure, you can make an egg white omelet with all the egg whites you're bound to have leftover from the other recipes in this cookbook, but this pavlova is so MATCHA better! Pavlova is a traditional dessert hailing from Australia and New Zealand featuring a meringue with a crisp exterior and soft, marshmallow-y interior. It's then typically topped with a sweetened whipped cream and fresh fruit. Here we're using a classic Japanese flavor combination of matcha and strawberries, with the addition of salted caramel to add a gooey texture and extra indulgence. This is an idea based on my own love for the combination of matcha and caramel—feel free to use this recipe as a jumping off point for your own pavlova by customizing the whipped cream and topping it with everything from fruit to chocolate and nuts.

Makes 1 large pavlova, halve the recipe to make 4 mini pavlovas

Meringue

4 large egg whites, room temperature

1 cup (200 g) caster sugar (substitute with granulated sugar pulsed in a blender or food processor)

1 tsp vinegar (white vinegar, white wine or apple cider)

½ tsp vanilla extract

1 tbsp (8 g) corn flour or cornstarch, sifted

Preheat the oven to 300°F (150°C) and prepare a sheet of parchment paper large enough to cover the bottom of an 8-inch (20-cm) or larger springform cake pan for a larger pavlova. You will use this as the base to shape the pavlova. Alternatively, you can trace a large bowl or plate onto the parchment paper to act as a guide. For mini pavlovas, use small bowls or saucers to trace four small, evenly-spaced circles on the parchment paper. Flip the sheet of parchment paper over so the side with pen/pencil is on the bottom and lay the paper on a baking tray and set aside.

Make the meringue. Place the egg whites in a large glass bowl or the bowl of a stand mixer. The mixing bowl and whisk attachment or electric hand blender need to be completely clean and dry; any oil residue will prevent the egg whites from turning into a meringue, so avoid using plastic bowls or whisks since those are more prone to having oil residue and use glass or stainless steel instead. Use an electric mixer or stand mixer to beat the egg whites on high speed for 2 minutes until stiff peaks begin to form. Gradually add about 1 tablespoon (13 g) of sugar at a time, beating for a few seconds after each addition. Once all the sugar is added, beat on high for another 5 minutes until it's thick, smooth, shiny and glossy.

Add the vinegar and vanilla extract before sifting the corn flour or starch directly into the bowl. Beat on low until just combined or use a rubber spatula to fold in the ingredients.

(continued)

Secure the parchment paper to the bottom of the springform pan or baking tray, that way it won't accidentally slip and ruin the shape of the pavlova when you move it to the oven. If using the bottom of a springform pan, flip it over so the raised edge is underneath and use a spatula to make tiny dollops of meringue near the edges of the flat side of the pan. If using a baking tray, place dollops underneath the edges of the parchment paper. Press the parchment paper into the dollops of meringue so the paper sticks to the spring form pan/baking tray.

Shape the pavlova. Pour the meringue into the center of the circle(s), distributing evenly between the four circles if making mini pavlovas, and use a rubber spatula to push the meringue to the edges of the circle. Now comes the fun part, where you can decide how you want your pavlova to look. To achieve the shape that's pictured on the large pavlova, use a spatula to press on the side of the circle and push the pavlova inward and upward like you're making big brush strokes, continuing to do this all the way around the pavlova until you have a volcano-like shape with deep grooves in it. You can also leave it more freeform by using a spatula to press in and out to make lots of little peaks all over the sides (like in the mini pavlovas pictured) or go the opposite route and smooth out the sides. Just make sure to shape it into a solid dome and use a spoon to make a small well in the center of the pavlova to hold the cream.

Carefully transfer the pavlova to the oven, then immediately turn the heat down to 225°F (110°C) and bake for 1 hour and 30 minutes for a large pavlova and 45 minutes to 1 hour for the small pavlovas, until they are crispy and very lightly golden on the outside. DO NOT open the oven door to check on it during this time. You don't want to make any drastic changes in the heat or else your pavlova will crack. After it's done baking, turn the oven off and leave it to cool gradually in the oven. DO NOT open the oven door, again to prevent cracking and deflating. Leave the larger pavlova there for at least 1 hour. For the mini pavlovas, you can remove them from the oven after 30 minutes then leave them to cool on a wire rack.

(continued)

MATCHA PAVLOVA (CONTINUED)

Salted Caramel

½ cup (100 g) granulated sugar

3 tbsp (42 g) unsalted butter, room temperature

¼ cup (60 ml) heavy cream or whipping cream, room temperature

¼–½ tsp fleur de sal, flaky sea salt like Maldon or sea salt

Matcha Cream

¾ cup (180 ml) cold heavy cream or whipping cream

1½ tbsp (24 g) caster sugar or granulated sugar, more to taste

½ tbsp (3 g) matcha powder (culinary grade preferred), more to taste

4–6 oz (114–170 g) fresh strawberries, hulled

Make the salted caramel while the pavlova is cooling. Heat the sugar in a saucepan over medium heat while stirring constantly with a heat-resistant rubber spatula or wooden spoon. Be patient—it will eventually melt into a golden-brown liquid as you continue stirring, usually 6 to 8 minutes. Make sure to keep stirring so it doesn't burn. The moment it has fully melted (it should be a nice amber color), carefully add the butter while stirring—watch out as it will bubble and may splatter when you add the butter. Once that's melted, let it cook without stirring for 1 minute, then remove it from the heat and slowly and carefully pour in the heavy cream—it will bubble again so be careful. Stir in the cream until it's fully incorporated, then let it boil for a minute and remove from the heat, stirring again until you have a smooth sauce. Mix in the salt then set it aside to cool while you prepare the other toppings.

Make the matcha whipped cream by beating the cold whipping cream, sugar and matcha powder on high until fluffy and spreadable, 2 to 3 minutes.

Prepare the strawberries. Put the de-stemmed side down on a cutting board and cut them in half or into thin slices, depending on how you want to present them.

Assemble the matcha pavlova by filling the well in the pavlova with matcha cream and spreading it out so it comes near the edges of the pavlova. Drizzle salted caramel all over, then top with strawberries and enjoy.

#MatchaPavlova #SweetTooth #IndulgentEatsatHome

MANGO FLOAT

My fellow mango lovers, this one's for you. While Thai mango sticky rice and Taiwanese mango shaved ice are some of my favorite ways to enjoy this tropical fruit, this popular Filipino dessert is the way I've eaten it the most throughout my life since it was always served at family gatherings. While the name "float" might imply a root beer float to some, the Filipino mango float is actually more like an icebox or no-bake cake. You simply layer all the ingredients in a container, stick it in the fridge and you have a decadent dessert to enjoy the next day, hence why Filipinos also refer to it as a "ref cake" (short for refrigerator, get it? 😊).

This can be made with fresh strawberries, canned peaches or your choice of fruit for a more budget-friendly version, but mango reigns supreme. It's my absolute favorite fruit, with Philippine mangoes being arguably the world's best thanks to their sweet and exotic flavor. Since mangoes are already sweet, I've adjusted the condensed milk to give you a bit of range if you prefer not-too-sweet desserts like I do. Either way, one bite is sure to transport you to the tropics. 😎

Makes a 1 (8-inch [20-cm]) square mango float

2 cups (250 g) graham crackers or Biscoff cookies

4 ripe mangoes, sliced or diced depending on what pattern you want to make

2 cups (480 ml) cold heavy whipping cream

7–14 oz (207–414 ml) sweetened condensed milk, depending on how sweet you want it

½ tsp pure vanilla extract

Crumble the graham crackers or Biscoff cookies by pulsing in a food processor or placing them in a resealable bag and smacking the crap out of them with a blunt object like a rolling pin.

Peel and cut the mangoes. Slice the mangoes in half, discarding the pits (but eat the mango on the edges first!). If you want to make a rose pattern as pictured, then cut long thin strips lengthwise. To dice the mangoes, cut a crosshair pattern into the mango and then scoop out the flesh. Feel free to get creative with the presentation! Set aside the cut mango while you work on the rest of the ingredients.

Make the whipped cream by whisking together the cream, condensed milk and vanilla extract by hand or with a mixer until thickened and doubled in size.

(continued)

MANGO FLOAT (CONTINUED)

Layer the ingredients in an 8-inch (20-cm) square baking dish if you're making one big serving or try using a smaller pan (like a 7-inch [18-cm] cake pan) along with a Mason jar—that way, you have a second individual serving that you can freeze and eat at a later time. Start by spreading an even layer with about a third of the whipped cream, then a third of the graham cracker crumbs, then a third of the mangoes and repeat until you have nine layers. If you are forming the rose pattern on top, start with the shorter pieces of mango to form concentric circles in the center, then keep swirling around to form the rose.

Cover or wrap in cling wrap and let it sit in the refrigerator for at least 8 hours before serving. If you want to freeze the cake for an ice cream–like texture or to serve at a later date, make sure to refrigerate it first so the graham cracker soaks in the cream before freezing—otherwise the graham crackers will stay hard.

Cut the float into slices and enjoy a taste of the Philippines.

#MangoFloat #SweetTooth #IndulgentEatsatHome

Be Prepared

♪ Be prepaaaared ♪ Fans of *The Lion King* will recognize this line from the classic song where Scar echoes those words to his pack of hyenas. While I'm not recommending that you engage in any malicious plots as he does in the movie, I AM hoping that line will get stuck in your head so you remember to always be prepared when making the recipes in this cookbook. So, what exactly do I mean when I say to be prepared?

#1—Most importantly, read every recipe all the way through prior to making them, so you won't be surprised to find out that you need a certain ingredient or that a later step requires overnight marination. Even better, scan the QR codes to watch the accompanying videos so you familiarize yourself with the techniques.

#2—Gather all the ingredients, utensils and equipment you'll need for a recipe ahead of time. There's nothing worse than getting noodles into boiling water or meat stewing, only to realize you're missing a key ingredient. You can access handy links to shop for many of the ingredients as well as the equipment you need through my digital kitchen essentials guide, which you can access via the QR code on page 230.

#3—Measure, chop and lay out all the ingredients in small containers near your cooking area BEFORE you start cooking (known as *mise en place* or "everything in its place"). The only exception is when I specifically call out the steps in a recipe where I recommend using waiting time to prep or chop ingredients, that way you can be as efficient with your time as possible—this is where Rule #1 comes in clutch! But putting in the work to organize everything ahead of time will save you a lot of headaches when managing cooking times.

Finally, make the recipes in this chapter! You'll notice these recipes mentioned as key ingredients for many of the earlier dishes. These recipes are the ultimate make-ahead upgrades, as all the components last a really long time in your fridge or freezer but deliver huge punches of flavor, so you can easily keep a batch handy to jazz up a wide variety of food. And while they can quickly be added to amp up a dish, most of these actually take quite a bit of time to prepare, whether in active cooking time like for the Caramelized Onion Cubes (page 220) or in waiting time like for the Pickled Goodness (page 223) and Salted Egg Yolks (page 226). So, carve out a night every week or so to make batches of the recipes in this chapter so you always have them at your disposal.

CARAMELIZED ONION CUBES

These cubes will change the way you cook! Caramelized onions are one of the best ingredients ever—simultaneously sweet, savory, jammy and luscious, they upgrade almost any dish they touch. But let's face it—it's a total PAIN to make caramelized onions. You have to start with a big bunch of onions, which will shrink down to less than half the volume, and you need to watch over your pan for almost a full hour to get that deep brown color and distinct flavor. Enter: caramelized onion cubes. The idea is that you make a huge batch of caramelized onions in one go and freeze them into ice cube–sized portions. This way, you can later add exactly the amount you need since ain't nobody got time to stand over a pot just to add a spoonful of caramelized onions to a breakfast sandwich! This recipe shows you how to cook four onions in one large pan to make 8 to 10 tablespoons (150 to 180 g) of caramelized onions to fill half a standard ice cube tray. I'd recommend making two batches at once by using two pans and starting one batch 5 to 10 minutes after the other so you'll have enough onions to make almost all the recipes in this cookbook!

Makes 8 to 10 tablespoons (150 to 180 g) caramelized onions

4 medium onions, peeled
4 tbsp (56 g) butter
2 tbsp (30 ml) olive oil
Salt, to taste

Prepare a cutting board area. Place a wet kitchen towel underneath the cutting board with the edges sticking out from underneath— this will prevent it from sliding around while you're slicing onions (do this every time you use a cutting board!). If you're a crier like me, the wet kitchen towel will ALSO perform double duty by preventing the tears! The acid in onions that irritates your eyes is drawn to moisture, so placing another source of moisture closer to the onions will prevent it from reaching your eyes, so make sure that the wet kitchen towel is sticking out along the edges of the cutting board.

Slice the onions. First, cut off the dirty roots, then cut the onions in half from the root through to the tip. Then, cut off the tip of the onion, which makes it easy to remove the peel. I also like to remove the outer, greenish layer of onion as I find that it doesn't caramelize well. Place the flat base of the onion down onto the cutting board and use the tip of the knife to remove the root by cutting a V-shape around the inner part of the root. Now make thin slices from root to tip, starting from one side all the way to the other, following the natural lines in the onion as a guide. Do this with all the onions—you will have a LOT, which is exactly what you want since they will shrink down as they cook.

Get a pan ready. You ideally want a pan with a wide base, thick bottom and high walls, that way there's lots of surface area for cooking, the heat is evenly distributed in the pan and the walls of the pan can keep the onions from flying out. I like to use both my Le Creuset braiser and Dutch oven to make two batches at once, but a high-walled skillet, a large saucepan or heavy-bottomed pot also work.

Heat the butter and olive oil over medium-high heat, then add the onions a large handful at a time, stirring to coat the onions in fat and waiting until the onions shrink a bit in volume before adding the next handful. Once all the onions are in and they're starting to soften, season with a pinch of salt.

Reduce the heat to medium-low and continue cooking while stirring every few minutes to make sure they cook evenly. They will start to turn a pale golden brown after 15 to 20 minutes, but it takes more time to get them super jammy and caramelized.

Continue cooking for another 20 to 30 minutes until you reach your desired level of caramelization, adding water as needed and as you see browned bits that stick to the bottom of the pan—this is known as fond and is what gives the onions amazing flavor, so make sure to use the water to loosen it so you can scrape it up and mix it into the onions. Regardless, you'll want to stir your onions every few minutes for even cooking, lowering the heat if needed to make sure the onions don't burn. I like my onions super brown and jammy, which takes about an hour of total cooking time, but you can also pull the onions from the heat a little early if you plan to cook them further down the line.

Serve immediately and prepare to store as ice cubes. Let the onions cool at room temperature before transferring into an ice cube tray. Once frozen, you can transfer the cubes to a freezer bag so you always have them on hand to defrost for the variety of recipes in this cookbook. You can also throw them straight from frozen into sauces and soups—just let your stove do its job to defrost and reheat the caramelized onions.

PICKLED GOODNESS

Tickle your tastebuds with homemade pickles! There are your standard dill pickles, but once you start pickling your own red onions and garlic, that's when the real fun begins! You'll be amazed at just how easy it is to create these little pops of bright acidic flavor that can transform your dish. For all these recipes, you can follow the same directions as all you need to do is fill a Mason jar with the vegetables you want to pickle and any spices or aromatics, then add its accompanying pickling liquid, stick it in the fridge and enjoy that pickled goodness in as quick as 30 minutes and for as long as 2 weeks!

Makes about 1 quart (400 g) of pickled veggies

Garlic Dill Pickles and Pickled Garlic (ready in the refrigerator in 24 hours)

3 pickling cucumbers or ½ Hot House cucumber, sliced into chips with a mandoline

5 sprigs dill

6 cloves garlic

½ tbsp (3 g) mustard seeds

½ tbsp (5 g) whole peppercorns

¼ onion, sliced

1–2 jalapeños

Garlic Dill Pickling Liquid

¾ cup (180 ml) white vinegar

1½ tsp (15 g) kosher salt

¼ tsp sugar

¼ cup (60 ml) water, plus more as needed

Pickled Red Onions (ready at room temperature in 1 hour, refrigerate overnight for more vibrant color)

1 large red onion, peeled and thinly sliced

1 clove garlic, optional

½ tsp whole black peppercorns, optional

1 dried bay leaf, optional

Red Onion Pickling Liquid

¾ cup (180 ml) apple cider vinegar

½ tsp kosher salt

¼ tsp sugar

Water, as needed

In a Mason jar, add the ingredients to be pickled to the jar, including all the spices, except for the pickling liquid.

Make the pickling liquid by heating the vinegar in a small pot with the salt and sugar, whisking until they dissolve. Add the water to the vinegar to cool it down, then pour the pickling liquid into the Mason jar. Add more water if needed to completely submerge the ingredients, then close the lid tightly and turn the jar upside down and back a few times to distribute the pickling liquid and spices.

Let it sit at room temperature or in the refrigerator for the directed times to the left and enjoy!

ROASTED GARLIC

Roasted garlic might be the most MVP ingredient in this cookbook. Unlike caramelized onions, which pay off big time but take a lot of effort, roasted garlic is insanely easy to make and almost foolproof. Just 40 minutes to an hour in the oven transforms the sharp flavor of raw garlic into a deep, sweet, caramelized and nutty version of garlic. It softens to the point that you can squeeze them right out of the peel, and a gentle press of a knife will instantly smush a clove into an almost creamy garlic paste that you can spread on toast. It blends easily to add flavor and body to sauces, like my Roasted Garlic Gochujang Mayo (page 106). Or you can enjoy them whole, adding those golden cloves on top of pizza or anything else you can think of. Keep it in an airtight container in the fridge for up to 2 weeks or in the freezer for up to 3 months so you always have it on hand to add a boost of flavor to your cooking.

Makes 1 or more heads of roasted garlic

1 or more heads garlic
1 or more tsp olive oil

Preheat the oven to 400°F (200°C) and make sure the rack is in the middle of the oven.

Peel the paper off the garlic, as much as you can. We're talking about the thin, papery outer layer—don't worry about the peel that's stuck to each individual clove. You want to leave those on so the whole head of garlic and all the cloves stay connected.

Slice the top off the head of garlic with a sharp knife. You want to cut enough to expose the top of every clove, ¼ to ½ inch (6 mm to 1.3 cm) from the top, then place the head(s) of garlic on a piece of foil big enough to wrap it, but don't wrap it just yet! First you need to drizzle the olive oil over the exposed tops of the garlic. This is the secret to roasting them to caramelized perfection. Now wrap up the garlic so it's fully covered in the foil.

Bake for 40 minutes to an hour until golden brown and completely soft in the center cloves. You can bake until you reach your desired level of caramelization—the longer you roast, the more golden brown and deep the flavor.

Let the garlic cool until it's safe to handle with your hands. Now you can squeeze the cloves right out of their peels to use in cooking, or let it cool completely at room temperature to then store in an airtight container in the fridge for up to 2 weeks or in the freezer for up to 3 months.

SALTED EGG YOLKS

If you don't have access to an Asian supermarket, then try making salted egg yolks at home! They are traditionally made by brining whole duck or chicken eggs in a saltwater solution or burying them in a salted ash for 6 to 8 weeks, but I wanted to show you the faster way that only uses the egg yolk. Salted egg whites are not as versatile, often being too salty to use in other dishes (though the Filipino salted egg salad that pairs it with tomatoes and onions is one nice exception). Here, we are curing just the yolks in salt to help preserve them, that way the raw egg whites can be repurposed for pavlova (page 211) and other egg white–based desserts, shaken into cocktails or whipped up into egg white omelets. You can actually freeze the egg whites in an ice cube tray too if you don't plan to use them within 2 days of making your salted egg yolks.

The important number to remember here is four—you will need at least 4 days to make the salted egg yolks, and I'd recommend making at least four egg yolks at a time so that you have enough to make one Golden Lava French Toast (page 35) and one serving of Salted Egg Prawns (page 143). It's the perfect Monday or Tuesday night activity so that the yolks are ready to use for weekend cooking fun. Double or triple this as needed depending on how many servings you're making! If you leave them to dry in the fridge even longer, they will harden so that you can grate them and use them wherever you might use Parmigiano since it has similar umami properties—think pasta and noodles (like my Umami Bomb Udon, [page 54]), rice (like Arroz Caldo, [page 167]), salads, chicken, etc. The salted egg yolks will keep in the fridge for at least 1 month—just use the good old smell test to see if they've gone bad.

Makes 4 to 12 salted egg yolks

Fine sea salt
4–12 egg yolks

Fill a wide airtight container with ¼ inch (6 mm) of fine sea salt, then use the back of a tablespoon to make a shallow well in the salt for each egg yolk with a small gap in between each well as you don't want the yolks touching.

Separate the egg yolks from the whites. I've found the easiest way to do this with the least risk of popping a yolk is by using your hands. First, prepare an airtight container to keep the clean egg whites in, a container with salt in it for the clean egg yolks and a small bowl for cracking the eggs over—just in case an egg breaks, you won't contaminate the clean egg whites/yolks. Crack an egg into the bowl and use clean hands to fish out the yolk, transferring the yolk between your fingers until the egg white is completely separated.

Gently use your hands to place each yolk into the wells you made in the container of salt. Now transfer the clean egg white from the bowl to the second airtight container and keep repeating this process until all the eggs are separated.

Cover the tops of the yolks with more salt so the surfaces of the yolks are fully coated in salt. You don't need to fill the entire thing so it's level, just enough so there's no unsalted parts of the yolk.

Cover and refrigerate for 24 hours. The yolks will harden into a sticky, gummy, dried apricot like disc—the wonders of salt-curing!

Wash off the salt under running water, then dry with paper towels and place it into a clean container wide enough so the yolks aren't touching. Cover loosely and leave in the refrigerator for another 3 days—this will help the yolks dry out. You can also choose to wrap them individually in cheese cloth and let them dry out for a full week, which will produce a hard consistency that allows you to grate the salted eggs onto dishes.

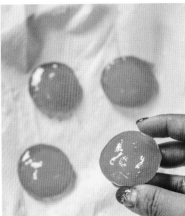

For use in French toast (page 35) and prawns (page 143), you need to cook the salted egg yolk. Steam for 15 minutes or until the egg yolks are a pale-yellow color all the way through, similar to a hard-boiled egg yolk. Now you can easily turn it into a powdery texture. You can mash the yolks at this consistency with forks or knives for use in recipes. Each salted egg yolk creates about 1 tablespoon (12 g) of mashed yolk.

SICHUAN CHILI CRISP OIL

Chili oil has been having a moment. Between cult favorites like the OG trend-starter Lao Gan Ma to my personal favorite Fly by Jing, plus countless versions from chefs, Trader Joe's® and everyone in between, there's no shortage of chili oil in the culinary universe. It adds delicious heat, texture and umami to practically everything: noodles, dumplings, fried chicken, popcorn, pizza and even ice cream. While it's easy to pick up a jar in the grocery store or online, it's nearly as easy but so much more satisfying to make it yourself at home. I could probably fall asleep to the soothing sounds of hot oil sizzling over chilis and spices.

Even better, you can customize it to match your own preferences for taste and sodium content. I like to keep the sodium level quite low so that you can add as much heat as you like to full-flavored dishes like my #SpicyPeanutNoods (page 48) or to soy-heavy sauces like my Spicy Tingly Pork Abura Soba (page 57) and the dipping sauce for my Gyoza Skillet (page 172). The sodium and umami I DO put in the chili comes from fermented black beans, the same soybeans that are used in your favorite Chinese black bean sauce dishes. They add a pop of salty goodness and can be found online or at your local Asian grocer. But if you want more of a stand-alone chili oil that can add both flavor and salt to dishes, throw in a chicken bouillon cube so you can infuse both salt and MSG into the oil itself.

Makes 1½ cups (360 ml) of chili crisp oil

1 cup (240 ml) peanut, canola or vegetable oil (I prefer peanut for flavor)

1–2 shallots, chopped

2 star anise

½ Chinese cinnamon stick

4–6 cloves garlic, minced

½–1 chicken bouillon cube, optional

½ tsp mushroom powder, optional

1 tsp sugar

1 tsp sesame seeds

1 (1-inch [2.5-cm]) piece ginger, minced

1½ tbsp (11 g) Chinese chili flakes, add more for extra spicy

1 tbsp (10 g) ground Sichuan peppercorn, add more for extra numbing

3–4 dried chilis (Sichuan erjingtiao chilis are my fave), broken into pieces

1 tbsp (15 g) fermented black beans or soybeans, optional

1 bay leaf, optional

Make the crispy bits by first heating the oil in a small saucepan over medium-low. Add the shallots, star anise and cinnamon stick. Cook for 5 minutes or until the shallots have just turned a light blonde color, turning the heat down to low once it begins to simmer. Add the garlic and cook for another 5 to 7 minutes until the crispy bits turn to a pale golden brown. The moment this happens, pour the crispy bits into a fine mesh strainer set over a heat-proof bowl or container to catch the oil, leaving it to cool completely so they stay crispy. Then reheat the oil with the chicken bouillon (if using) over medium heat to 350°F (176°C), or until bubbles form around a wooden chopstick stuck into the oil.

If you don't care about getting the bits crispy, just heat the oil along with the chicken bouillon (if using) to 350°F (176°C). You will add the garlic, shallot, star anise and cinnamon stick with the rest of the ingredients in the next step. They will still add a ton of flavor even if they aren't crispy.

In a ceramic bowl or heatproof glass container, combine the mushroom powder (if using), sugar, sesame seeds, ginger, chili flakes, peppercorn, dried chilis, beans (if using) and bay leaf (if using). Pour the hot oil onto the other chili oil ingredients—listen to that sizzle! Let the oil cool until you can safely touch it, then add your crispy bits to the oil.

Use immediately or transfer to a glass jar and let it all sit for a few hours or overnight, so the flavors really infuse into the oil. Put it on EVERYTHING.

Kitchen Essentials

Learning the techniques for how to braise, deep-fry, steam dumplings or make meringue is only half the battle. To be able to execute all the recipes in this cookbook with ease, it helps to have the right equipment for each of these jobs. While I've tried to include ways to complete tasks with different types of cookware or by hand, it will make your life easier if you have the essentials pictured here.

Scan the QR code to watch a video where I go through all the tools and appliances that will bring you the most success in cooking your way through this book, with snippets showing how I use each piece in specific recipes.

The top three pans you need are:

1. **A good, high-walled nonstick skillet with a lid,** which can be used to make all kinds of eggs, jiggly pancakes (page 42) and all of the panfried dumplings in #PocketsofLove (page 171). It functions as a replacement for a wok to make fried rice and stir-fried dishes if you don't own one (though I highly recommend you also invest in a wok if you have the space for it!). The skillet can also be used to braise food, though an enameled cast-iron braiser works best for this type of task if you're able to invest in one.

2. **A cast-iron skillet,** which is best for obtaining that desired crust on mac and cheese and my crispy skillet pizza (page 83), along with creating a hard sear on meats and acting as the perfect vessel for sizzling sisig pictured to the left (page 111) and Bolognese with Cheesy Garlic Bombs (page 119).

3. **A pot with a lid to cook sauces, rice, pasta and more,** though if you can invest in a Dutch oven, it will serve you even better. This enameled cast-iron pot goes from stove to oven to table for serving, and has a tight-fitting lid perfect for making Birria de Res (page 113) and Jollof Rice pictured to the left (page 163). They also retain heat well, making them perfect vessels for deep-frying.

You also want to have a good set of sharp knives, a wooden spoon, a ladle, both a plastic and metal spatula, a slotted spoon and tongs. If you're deep-frying, it's also incredibly useful to have a spider, which is a type of strainer with a long handle that makes it easy to scoop food out of a deep pot while letting the oil or water drain out through its holes. A regular fine mesh strainer is also critical for straining impurities out of the oil when you're done with it, that way you can reuse leftover frying oil—strainers also work double duty, since you can use them to sift flour. Finally, a box grater and Microplane® are critical for being able to shred and grate cheese off the block.

If you plan to do any baking, an electric hand mixer or a stand mixer will save you so much time and energy, rather than whisking or kneading things by hand. For making my giant gooey cookies (page 207), it's almost impossible to get the same result without one of these pieces of equipment since you need to cream softened butter and sugar together to get the right texture in the final cookies, so I highly recommend investing in these if you want to bake them. A kitchen scale is also incredibly handy for weighing out ingredients for baking and making doughs.

My other essential appliances are a food processor or chopper, blender and air fryer. As you can tell in reading through my recipes, the food processor helps so much with chopping and mincing vegetables. It can complete the 5-minute job of mincing a head of garlic in 10 seconds and saves you so much time when making dumpling fillings. It also helps to have a blender for making the various dipping sauces throughout my cookbook, though you can also use a food processor for many of these jobs. If you follow me on Instagram, you know how obsessed I am with my air fryer. I've included air fryer cooking methods for many of the recipes in this book if you want to cut down on how much oil you consume or speed up baking times.

This is a high-level list of the essentials you need for my cookbook, but I highly recommend picking up a copy of J. Kenji Lopez-Alt's book *The Food Lab* and reading through his in-depth guide on essential kitchen gear. It's got all the information you need along with scientific explanations behind how different types of cookware work so you can really get your kitchen fully equipped to complete all forms of cooking. It's also an insanely useful cookbook to help you master all the basics of cooking and learn new techniques. He's one of many people who you should follow to expand your knowledge of cooking. Flip the page for more inspiring creators and chefs 👉.

Diversify Your Feed

Below, you'll find my favorite chefs, content creators, media platforms and experts who informed and influenced the recipes in this cookbook. Give them a follow to discover new perspectives and dive deeper into the cuisines you just cooked!

All Around
@inagarten
@nigellalawson
@davidchang
@ciaosamin
@kenjilopezalt
@sohlae
@bingingwithbabish
@cooksillustrated
@food52
@thefeedfeed

Baking & Dessert
@chelsweets
@bromabakery
@kingarthurbaking
@devamadeo
@hummingbirdhigh
@nm_meiyee
@sallysbakeblog

Black/African Diaspora
@chefkwameonwuachi
@immaculatebites
@chefjj
@yewande_komolafe
@9jafoodie
@shelinacooks

Chinese
@omnivorescookbook
@woksoflife
@hellolisalin
@eatchofood
@chinesecookingdemystified
@nom_life

Eastern European
@annavoloshynacooks
@foodloversdiary
@oliahercules

Italian & Italian-American
@massimobottura
@frankprinsinzano
@chefanthony_ballatosnyc
@saltyseattle
@the_pastaqueen
@pastasocialclub
@pastagrannies

Filipino
@fork_knife
@nicoleponseca
@filipinofoodmovement
@foxyfolksy
@chefjayps
@tenthousandthspoon
@filipinofoodcrawl

Grilling & Meat
@angiekmar
@chefcapon
@overthefirecooking
@maxthemeatguy

Japanese
@justonecookbook
@chopstickchronicles
@ramentology
@ramenjunkie
@sushiartisan

Korean
@maangchi
@choibites
@chefchrischo
@thekoreanvegan
@chefchrisoh
@jamesyworld

Mexican
@enriqueolveraf
@alexstupak
@mexicoinmykitchen
@happybelliesbyjenny

Mediterranean
@themediterraneandish
@dianekochilas

Middle Eastern
@ottolenghi
@adeenasussman
@chefeinat
@jakecohen
@anisagrams
@mybigfathalalblog_

Pizza
@mamas_too
@danieleuditi
@adamkuban
@lucali_bk
@oonihq

Plant-Based
@chez.jorge
@thefoodietakesflight
@iamtabithabrown
@woon.heng
@sweetpotatosoul

South Asian
@padmalakshmi
@priyakrishna
@pakistaneats
@thunapahadiaries
@himalayandumplings

Southeast Asian
@marionskitchen
@hotthaikitchen
@rasamalaysia
@danielfooddiary

Spanish & Portuguese
@chefjoseandres
@chefjosegarces
@joseavillez

Vietnamese
@andreanguyen88
@lukenguyencooks
@twaydabae
@johnnguyy

Thanks a Million

To Mike Profeta—you are my everything. You've dealt with the freakouts, been my hand model and sometimes even my photographer, slept alone until I would finally crawl to bed at 5:00 a.m. after long nights of editing and everything in between. I couldn't have done this without your patience, humor and unwavering support—I love you.

To Mom and Dad—you inspired my love for food and supported me through leaving a high-paying corporate job to pursue my passions. I will never take that or all your sacrifices along the way for granted and love you both so much.

To Josa Balisi—the best sister in the world. I could never have gotten to this point without your advice, support and, let's face it, superior memory and organization skills. I love you 3000.

To Liza Chegyem—you are our indispensable hero. Thank you for helping us clean up our apartment after my recipe testing tornado wreaked its destruction every few days.

To Cher Cresner—my Taobao queen. My recipes and photography wouldn't be possible without your help ordering equipment and props.

To Derry Ainsworth—photographer and videographer extraordinaire. Thanks for making me look way more professional than I feel and for all the dope photos over the years.

To Lyle Fernandez and Christy Verheij—thank you for lending me your beautiful kitchen for my photos and for your company during such a hectic shoot.

To Alexandra Strimbu—thank you for holding down the fort and helping me capture and edit New York content while I was slammed with cookbook work.

To my taste testers—Betty Ban, Bobby Rubino, Brandon Crowfeather, Chui Wong, Claudia Enriquez, Connor Quinn, Dave Guo, Ellis Johnstone, Elliot Faber, Erik Hellquivst, Flora Ma, Iris Yang, Jeanette Smerin, Karen Tang, Karolis Adomaitis, Kate Hicks, Katrina Oropel, Kevin O'Toole, Marina Misisca, Mark Meehan, Mark Wolfson, Mat Lee, Nadeem Hussain, Olivier Klein, Rich Smerin, Richie Hornung, Samantha Lin, Sandeep Sagoo, Therese Lee, Tiffany Faber, Tim Cresner and Vivian Gu—thanks for your valuable feedback, hungry mouths to help me not waste food while recipe testing and, most importantly, the wonderful company!

To my recipe testers, from my dear friends to my followers—Amy Kaneko, Anson Ma, Chloe Rogers, Constance Leung, Daniela Karadzhova, Dora Perera, Emma Carney, Faith Santiago, Gian Manalili, Heidi Wong, Jacqueline Chan, Karen Wang, Kasey Romero, Kristen Fisher, Kyla Kelly, Menchie Mana-ay, Nicole Rodriguez, Petrina Chan, Ryan Eldridge, Shirley Vu, Stephanie Chan, Terrence Gray and Valerie Chan—thanks for being the first to turn my recipes into real life dishes! Your feedback and enthusiasm informed so much of this book.

To the Hong Kong food purveyors, delivery services and restaurants that provided many of the high-quality ingredients used for my recipes–Argyle Black, Carbs HK, Feather & Bone, FINI's, Foodpanda Hong Kong, Posto Pubblico, Silencio, The Italian Club, Quezon Pinoy, Waves Pacific—many of these recipes and especially photos wouldn't be possible without your help, so thank you!

To Emily Taylor, William Kiester and the team at Page Street Publishing—thank you for your guidance, patience and, most importantly, for believing in me and my vision. I'm eternally grateful and so proud of what we've accomplished.

And most importantly, to all of you reading this, THANK YOU SO MUCH for supporting me and my lifelong dream of creating my very own cookbook. I hope these pages and the recipes you cooked brought you happiness. I'm eternally grateful that you've allowed me to pursue my passions, and I hope that passion has been apparent and inspires you in your own life.

About the Author

JEN BALISI is the founder of Indulgent Eats, sharing her globally-inspired cooking, dining and travel adventures to over 400,000 hungry fans across Instagram, her blog and YouTube. Jen's drool-worthy videos of delicious original recipes and mind-blowing menu items have reached millions of people around the globe, earning her features on Eater, BuzzFeed, Thrillist, HuffPost and more.

While Jen attempts bi-continental living with regular visits back home to New York City, she spends most of the year in Hong Kong where she's happily lived since 2017 with her husband and goldendoodle. When Jen's not taking advantage of Hong Kong's short flights to the Philippines and other parts of Asia, she's cooking and hosting friends for dinner parties and game nights, breaking a sweat at the gym or on a hike, staying up until the wee hours at bars and clubs and exploring Hong Kong's vibrant dining scene.

Index